Historical Outlines Of English Phonology And Middle English Grammar

Samuel Moore

In the interest of creating a more extensive selection of rare historical book reprints, we have chosen to reproduce this title even though it may possibly have occasional imperfections such as missing and blurred pages, missing text, poor pictures, markings, dark backgrounds and other reproduction issues beyond our control. Because this work is culturally important, we have made it available as a part of our commitment to protecting, preserving and promoting the world's literature. Thank you for your understanding.

Historical Outlines of English Phonology
and
Middle English Grammar

FOR COURSES IN CHAUCER, MIDDLE ENGLISH,
AND THE HISTORY OF THE ENGLISH LANGUAGE

By

SAMUEL MOORE

*Associate Professor of English in the
University of Michigan*

GEORGE WAHR
ANN ARBOR, MICHIGAN
1919

Copyright 1919
By
Samuel Moore

PRINTED AND BOUND BY
GEORGE BANTA PUBLISHING COMPANY
MANUFACTURING PUBLISHERS
MENASHA, WISCONSIN

PREFACE

Inasmuch as this book is intended for use in three distinct courses of the English curriculum—Chaucer, Middle English, and the history of the English language—I hope I may be permitted a few words of explanation as to the purpose its various parts are intended to serve in relation to these courses.

The elementary course in Chaucer is usually the student's introduction both to the study of medieval literature and to the study of Middle English. There will always, probably, be difference of opinion as to the relative emphasis that should be placed on these two aspects of the course, but its content must always be to some extent linguistic. All teachers desire that their students shall learn to read Chaucer aloud with a facility comparable to that with which they read a modern poet and with a fair degree of approximation to Chaucer's own pronunciation, and most teachers desire that they shall acquire some notion of the organic value of final *e* in Chaucer's language. The purpose of Part II of this book is to enable the elementary student to acquire a sound and accurate knowledge of Chaucer's language without the expenditure of an inordinate amount of time, and to arouse the student's interest in this part of his work by emphasising the principles that are illustrated in the study of Chaucer's language. The treatment of the subject is intended to be thoroly clear to students who have not studied Old English, and yet to give such students some degree of real understanding of the relation of Chaucer's language to Old English on the one hand and to Modern English on the other.

Of all the languages taught in our universities Middle English furnishes the best material for the study of language in the making, for the direct observation of linguistic change; yet the pedagogical difficulties involved in emphasising adequately this aspect of the study of Middle English are such that our courses in Middle English have tended on the whole to become mere translation courses. In Part IV of this book, dealing with the historical development of Middle English inflections, I have tried to unify for the student the apparent confusion of Early Middle English forms by showing in detail how Old English developed into the Middle English of Chaucer thru the action of the two great causes of change in language, sound change and analogy. The study of Part IV is prepared for by the account of the history of English sounds which is contained in Part III, and it is supplemented by the account of the Middle English dialects which is contained in Part V. Parts III, IV, and V, like Part II, are intended to be thoroly clear to students who have not studied Old English, but they are equally well adapted to the needs of the student who has studied Old English.

The course in the history of the English language is usually intended for students who have studied neither Old English nor Middle English, and for that reason it presents certain difficulties for the teacher. The greatest difficulty is that of enabling such students to acquire anything approaching a clear and definite knowledge of the changes of pronunciation that have taken place in English during the past thousand years. The best method, I believe, of meeting this difficulty is to begin the study of English phonology with the phonetic analysis of the student's own speech, this analysis being accompanied by and based upon a study of the elements of phonetics and practice in the use of a phonetic alphabet. If then the Old English, Middle English, and Modern English words that illustrate English sound changes are interpreted by means of the phonetic alphabet which the student has learned, he can gain from a study of them such a knowledge of the history of English sounds as he could not possibly gain from a study of the same words in their ordinary spellings. The Introduction to this book, dealing with the elements of phonetics, Part I, dealing with Modern English sounds, and Part III, dealing with the history of English sounds, furnish material for the study of English phonology according to this method. The study of the history of English inflections may be based on Part IV, which deals with the historical development of Middle English inflections, for, tho the inflections of Modern English are outside the scope of this book, it is not difficult to show the student that the Modern English forms are virtually those of Late Middle English minus the final *e* which was lost in the fifteenth century.

The phonetic notation I have used in this book is a modification of that of the International Phonetic Alphabet. Practical considerations, however, have led me to depart from the International alphabet farther than I originally intended. For the purposes of this book it seemed clearly desirable to use as the sign of vowel length the macron which is used by editors of Old and Middle English texts rather than the colon of the International alphabet. There seemed also to be a distinct advantage in using as the symbols of "open *o*" and "open *e*" the characters ǫ and ę which are used in Middle English texts rather than the International symbols. Some persons may possibly object to my use of ē and ō as symbols for the vowel sounds of Modern English *they* and *low*. My primary reason for using these symbols rather than symbols that indicate the diphthongal nature of these vowels is that the amount and kind of diphthongisation of these and other "long vowels" is by no means uniform in American English. It therefore seemed best to use ē, ō, etc. as somewhat conventional symbols for these sounds and to explain their diphthongal nature at appropriate places in the footnotes.

It would be impossible for me to acknowledge my indebtedness to all the sources I have used in the preparation of this book, but I know that I am under particular obligations to Sweet's *History of English Sounds, New English Grammar, First Middle English Primer, Second Middle English Primer, Sounds of English,* and *Primer of Spoken English*; Jespersen's *Progress in Language with Special Reference to English* and *Modern English Grammar*, Part I (*Sounds and Spellings*); Wyld's *Historical Study of the Mother Tongue* and *Short History of English*; Grandgent's *English in America* (*Die Neueren Sprachen*, II, 443 ff., 520 ff.); Morsbach's *Mittelenglische Grammatik*; Kaluza's *Historische Grammatik der englischen Sprache*; Stratmann's *Middle English Dictionary* (revised by Bradley); Emerson's *Middle English Reader*; Child's *Observations on the Language of Chaucer*; Kittredge's *Observations on the Language of Chaucer's Troilus*; Ten Brink's *Language and Metre of Chaucer* (translated by Smith); Liddell's grammatical introduction to his edition of Chaucer's *Prologue to the Canterbury Tales, Knightes Tale*, etc.; Skeat's *Complete Works of Geoffrey Chaucer* (Oxford, 6 vols.); Cromie's *Ryme-Index to the Ellesmere Manuscript of Chaucer's Canterbury Tales*; and Hempl's *Chaucer's Pronunciation*.

I am much indebted to my colleague Prof. W. R. Humphreys for help he has given me in reading proof.

I need scarcely say that I shall be grateful to those who will call my attention to any omissions or errors which they may observe in their use of this book or who can suggest any changes by which it may be better adapted to the purposes for which it is intended.

S. M.

CONTENTS

Introduction: The Elements of Phonetics 1

Part I Modern English Sounds 6

Part II The Language of Chaucer

    Pronunciation 12
    Inflections 25
    Final e 32

Part III The History of English Sounds

    Pronunciation of Old English 36
    Normal Development of Old English Vowels in ME and MnE 38
    Special Developments in Middle English 40
    Special Developments in Modern English 43
    Consonant Sounds 47

Part IV Historical Development of Middle English Inflections

    Nouns 49
    Adjectives 55
    Pronouns 57
    Verbs 60

Part V Middle English Dialects

    Distribution 71
    Southern Dialect 71
    Kentish Dialect 73
    Midland Dialect 74
    Non-Northern Dialect Characteristics 75
    Non-Southern Dialect Characteristics 76
    Northern Dialect 77

Appendix: Middle English Spelling 79

INTRODUCTION

THE ELEMENTS OF PHONETICS

1. Organs of Speech. Speech-sounds are produced by a stream of air expelled from the lungs, which is modified in various ways by means of the larynx, containing the vocal cords; the soft palate; the hard palate; the teeth; the lips; the tongue; and the nasal passage. The hard and soft palates form the roof of the mouth, the hard palate being in front, the soft palate behind. By the varied activity of these organs, the various consonant and vowel sounds are produced.

2. Voiced and Voiceless Sounds. With reference to the activity of the vocal cords, sounds are either voiced or voiceless. All speech sounds are produced by the expulsion of a stream of air from the lungs. In the production of a voiceless or breath sound, the stream of air passes freely thru the larynx; the vocal cords are wide open, so that they offer no impediment to the stream of air and therefore do not vibrate. But in the production of a voiced sound, the vocal cords are drawn close together so that they are caused to vibrate by the stream of air which passes between them. This vibration can be felt by placing the first two fingers upon the larynx or "Adam's apple" while one is pronouncing a vowel sound, or the consonant **v**. All vowel sounds are voiced, but consonants may be either voiced or voiceless. It is voice that distinguishes **g** (as in *get*) from **k**, **d** from **t**, **b** from **p**, **v** from **f**, **z** from **s** (as in *soon*), and the sound of **th** in *then* from the sound of **th** in *thin*.[1]

3. Stops and Spirants. With reference to the manner of their articulation, consonants are distinguished as stopped consonants (or explosives)

---

[1] By practice one may soon learn to distinguish voiced sounds from voiceless ones. A good exercise for practice is to pronounce alternately **s** and **z**, **f** and **v**, and the two sounds of **th**, taking care to pronounce the consonant sound alone without the aid of a vowel. The sounds of **t** and **d**, **p** and **b**, etc., when pronounced without a vowel, will also be felt and heard to be very different in character. It will also be observed that voiced sounds, whether vowels or consonants, are capable of being uttered with variations of musical pitch, whereas voiceless sounds are not. Of the following sounds, distinguish those that are voiced from those that are not: **l, m, n, r, sh.**

and open consonants (or spirants). In the production of stopped consonants, the outgo of breath from the lungs is stopped at some point by the complete closing of the mouth passage. The increasing pressure of the breath then forces open the stoppage, causing an explosive sound. In the production of open consonants or spirants, the mouth passage is not completely stopped, but the air from the lungs is made to pass thru a narrow opening with so much friction as to cause a buzzing or hissing noise. Stopped consonants are Modern English **g** (as in *get*), **k, d, t, b, p**; open consonants are **z, s, th** (as in *then*), **th** (as in *thin*), **v, f**.[1]

4. The complete or partial closure required to produce stops and open consonants is made by means of the tongue or lips, and the quality of the various sounds is determined by the manner in which the closure is made. Modern English **g** (as in *get*) and **k** are produced by pressure of the tongue against the soft palate; **y** (as in *yield*), is made by an incomplete closure between the tongue and the hard palate; **d** and **t** are made by the pressure of the front of the tongue against the ridge above the upper front teeth; **z** and **s** are made with an incomplete closure at the same point; **b** and **p** are produced by means of a closure of the two lips; **v** and **f** are produced by an incomplete closure between the lower lip and the upper front teeth; **th** as in *then*, and **th** as in *thin* are produced by causing air to pass between the tip of the tongue and the backs or edges of the upper front teeth.

5. According to the place of their formation, these consonants are therefore classified as back or velar consonants (**g, k**); front or palatal consonants (**y**); dental consonants (**d, t, z, s, th** in *then*, **th** in *thin*); and labial consonants (**b, p, v, f**).

6. **Nasal and Oral Consonants.** With reference to the activity of the nasal passage, consonants are classified as oral or nasal. All of the consonants mentioned in the preceding paragraph are oral consonants. The nasal consonants are **m, n,** and **ng** (as in *thing*). In the articulation of the oral consonants, the passage from the throat to the nose is closed, so that the steam of air emitted by the lungs can escape only thru the mouth. In the articulation of the nasal consonants, however, the passage from the throat to the nose is left open, so that air can escape freely thru the nose.

---

[1] Are **r, sh,** and **y** open consonants or stopped consonants?

At the same time the mouth passage is completely stopped, the closure being made for **m**, **n**, and **ng**, precisely as for **b**, **d**, and **g**, respectively.[3]

7. Vowels. Vowel sounds are more open than open consonant sounds. In the formation of an open consonant, a stream of air is made to pass thru an opening so narrow that the passage of the air causes friction and therefore noise. In the formation of a vowel, however, the opening is so wide that the air in passing thru the mouth causes no friction at all.

8. Open and Close Vowels. But the vowels are not all equally open in their formation. If one pronounces in order the vowel sounds of the words **hat, hate, heat**, he will observe that in pronouncing each of these successive sounds the tongue is closer to the roof of the mouth. When we pronounce the series, the tongue starts from a position considerably below the roof of the mouth and ends in a position quite close to the roof of the mouth. This can be felt, and it can also be seen by pronouncing the sounds before a mirror. The same thing can be observed in regard to the vowels of the words **law, low, loot**. As we pronounce this series of vowels, we can feel the tongue going higher in the mouth, and we can see it indirectly by watching the upward movement of the lower jaw as we pronounce the three sounds before a mirror.

9. This difference in openness or height is the basis of one of the most important classifications of vowel sounds. We distinguish at least three degrees in the height of vowel sounds. If the tongue is quite close to the roof of the mouth, we call the vowel a **high** vowel. If the tongue occupies a low position in the mouth, we call the vowel a **low** vowel. If the tongue is in a position about midway between its extreme high position and its extreme low position, we call the vowel a **mid** vowel. So the vowels of **law** and **hat** are **low** vowels, the vowels of **low** and **hate** are **mid** vowels, and the vowels of **loot** and **heat** are **high** vowels.

10. Back and Front Vowels. When we pronounce in succession the two series of vowels heard in *law, low, loot*, and *hat, hate, heat*, we can perceive that the tongue lies differently as we utter the two series. When we pronounce the vowels of *law, low, loot*, it is the **back** of the tongue that is closest to the roof of the mouth. When we pronounce the vowels of

---

[3] Vowels are normally oral sounds, but they become nasalized when they are pronounced with the passage from the throat to the nose open. The most familiar examples of nasalized vowels are those of Modern French.

hat, hate, heat, it is the **front** of the tongue that is closest to the roof of the mouth. This can be felt, and it can also be seen by looking into the mouth as we pronounce the two series of sounds before a mirror. We therefore call the vowels of *law, low, loot,* **back** vowels, and the vowels of *hat, hate, heat* **front** vowels. This is the second basis of the classification of vowel sounds.

11. Combining the two classifications of vowel sounds, we say that the vowel of **hat** is a **low front** vowel, that the vowel of **hate** is a **mid front** vowel, that the vowel of **heat** is a **high front** vowel, that the vowel of **law** is a **low back** vowel, that the vowel of **low** is a **mid back** vowel, and that the vowel of **loot** is a **high back** vowel.[4]

12. Round and Unround Vowels. If one pronounces before a mirror the two series of vowel sounds heard in *hat, hate, heat,* and *law, low, loot,* he will see that the action of the lips in pronouncing the two series is not the same. In pronouncing the first series, the corners of the mouth are drawn apart so as to make a wide opening. But in pronouncing the latter series, the corners of the mouth are drawn together so as to make a more or less rounded opening; in fact, one finds that he cannot pronounce this series of vowels with the corners of the mouth drawn apart. We therefore make a further distinction between round and unround vowels, and call the vowel of **law** a **low back round** vowel, the vowel of **low** a **mid back round** vowel, and the vowel of **loot** a **high back round** vowel. The vowels of **hat, hate, heat,** on the other hand, are unround vowels.

13. Generally speaking, back vowels tend to be round, and front vowels to be unround. But unround back vowels and round front vowels also occur. The vowel of Modern English *far* is a mid back unround vowel. Front round vowels may be illustrated by Modern German *kühn* and *müssen*, in which are heard the long and short varieties of the high front round vowel. The vowel of *kühn* may be produced by pronouncing the vowel of *heat* with the lips rounded as if for pronouncing the vowel of *loot*. The vowel of *müssen* may be produced by pronouncing the vowel of *hit* with the lips rounded as if for pronouncing the vowel of *pull*. No front round vowels occur in Modern English, but the two sounds just described were frequent sounds in Old English.

---

[4] Some vowels, for example a in English *Cuba*, e in German *gabe*, e in French *je*, are neither front vowels nor back vowels. They occur chiefly in unstressed syllables and are generally termed mixed vowels.

14. Quantity of Vowels. The foregoing classification of vowel sounds has reference only to the **quality** of vowels. But vowels differ from each other not only in quality but also in **quanitiy** or length of duration. With regard to quantity, vowels are distinguished as **long** and **short**.[1] In Modern English the long vowel of **meet** differs from the short vowel of **met** not only in quantity but also in quality, the former being a high front vowel and the latter a mid front vowel. Likewise, the long vowel in **loot** differs from the short vowel in **look** both in quality and in quantity; both vowels are high back round vowels, but the latter is slightly lower or more open in its formation than the former. On the other hand, the long vowel of **art** differs from the vowel of the first syllable of **artistic** in length or duration alone.

15. Diphthongs. A diphthong consists of two vowel sounds pronounced in a single syllable. In Modern English we have diphthongs in the words *foil, foul,* and *file.*

---

[1] The student must guard against the phonetically incorrect use of the terms **long** and **short** as they are applied in modern English dictionaries. The vowel in *mate* is called "long a," the vowel in *mat* is called "short a"; but the two vowels are not the long and short varieties of one sound; they differ in quality as well as in length.

PART I

MODERN ENGLISH SOUNDS

16. Phonetic Alphabet. The sounds of Modern English are expressed in phonetic notation as follows:

ā	like	a	in	father
a	”	a	”	artistic, o in fodder
æ	”	a	”	hat
b	”	b	”	be
d	”	d	”	do
ē	”	a	”	mate
eͤ	”	a	”	chaotic
ę̄	”	ai	”	airy
ę	”	e	”	met
f	”	f	”	fee
g	”	g	”	go
h	”	h	”	heed
ī	”	i	”	machine
i	”	i	”	bit
iͤ	”	ia	”	carriage
j	”	y	”	yes
k	”	k	”	kin
l	”	l	”	let
m	”	m	”	meet
n	”	n	”	net
ŋ	”	ng	”	sing
ō	”	o	”	note
oͤ	”	o	”	donation
ǭ	”	a	”	all
ǭͤ	”	au	”	audacious
p	”	p	”	pit
r	”	r	”	rat
s	”	s	”	seat
ʃ	”	sh	”	ship

ͤ This sound occurs only in unstressed syllables and in syllables with secondary stress; it does not occur in strongly stressed syllables.

ʒ	like	s	in	plea**s**ure
t	"	t	"	**t**one
þ	"	th	"	**th**in
ð	"	th	"	**th**en
ū	"	oo	"	b**oo**t
u	"	u	"	p**u**sh
ʌ	"	u	"	h**u**t
ɔ̄	"	u	"	**u**rge
ə⁶	"	a	"	**a**bout
v	"	v	"	**v**at
w	"	w	"	**w**in
z	"	z	"	**z**est

Dipththongs:

ai	"	i	"	f**i**nd
au	"	ou	"	**ou**'
jū } iu	"	u	"	acc**u**se, m**u**te
ju⁶	"	u	"	acc**u**sation
ǫi	"	oy	"	b**oy**

Consonant combinations:

hw	"	wh	in	**wh**y
tʃ	"	ch	"	**ch**ew
dʒ	"	j	"	**j**aw

For the representation of certain sounds which occurred in Old English and Middle English, but which do not occur in Modern English, the following additional characters are needed:

h before consonants and after vowels like ch in German i**ch**, na**ch**t⁷

ȝ			" g "	North German sa**g**en	
ȳ			" üh "	German k**üh**n	
y			" ü "	"	m**ü**ssen
œ̄			" ö "	"	h**ö**ren
œ			" ö "	"	w**ö**rter

⁶ This sound occurs only in unstressed syllables and in syllables with secondary stress; it does not occur in strongly stressed syllables.

⁷ The sounds of ch which occur in German *ich* and *nacht* are of course altogether different from the sound of h in *heed*, and are usually represented in phonetic notation by the characters ç and x respectively. The character h is used in our alphabet merely for the sake of simplicity.

17. **Keywords.** The Modern English key-words given above are written in phonetic notation as follows:

fɑðər	gō	nŏt	ðęn	ækjūz, ækiuz[a]
artistĭk	hĭd	donēʃən	bŭt	mjūt, miut[a]
fadər	məʃĭn	ǫl	puʃ	ækjuzēʃən
hæt	bit	ǫdēʃəs	hʌt	bǫi
bĭ	kærĭdẓ	pit	ɜrdẓ	hwai
dū	jęs	ræt	əbaut	tʃū
mĕt	kin	sĭt	væt	dẓǭ
keatĭk	lęt	ʃip	win	
ęrĭ	mĭt	plęẓər	zęst	
męt	nęt	tŏn	faind	
fĭ	siŋ	þin	aut	

18. **Modern English in Phonetic Notation.** The pronunciation represented in the paragraphs printed below is the natural pronunciation of the transcriber (who is a native of southeastern Pennsylvania) when speaking at a rate about midway between slow, formal speech and rapid, colloquial speech. In the transcriber's dialect the vowel [ə][9a] is extremely frequent and occurs in many situations where speakers from other localities would use [ĭ]. In studying the transcription the student should observe that many words, especially pronouns, prepositions, and auxiliary verbs, have "strong" and "weak" forms. The strong forms are used when these words are strongly stressed, the weak forms are used when they are weakly stressed. For example, the strong form of *who* is [hū], the weak form is [hu] or [u]. The student should also observe that r, l, m, and n often form a syllable even when they are not accompanied by a vowel; they do so, for example, in [**papjəl'r**], line 7; [**pipl̩**], line 7; and [**kanvərsēʃn**], line 3. Syllabic r, l, m, and n, when necessary for clearness, are written ['r], ['l̩], ['m̩], and ['n̩]. In the conventional spelling the first paragraph of the text transcribed below is as follows:

In every cultivated language there are two great classes of words which, taken together, comprise the whole vocabulary. First, there are those words with which we become acquainted in ordinary conversation,—which we learn, that is to say, from the members of our own family

---

[a] Both pronunciations occur in American English.

[9a] Here and elsewhere the brackets are used to indicate that the spellings they enclose are phonetic spellings.

and from our familiar associates, and which we should know and use even if we could not read or write. They concern the common things of life and are the stock in trade of all who speak the language. Such words may be called "popular," since they belong to the people at large and are not the exclusive possession of a limited class.

ɪn ęvrɪ kʌltəvetəd lęŋgwɪdʒ ðęr ər tū grēt klæsəz əv wɜrdz hwɪtʃ, tēkn təgęðər, kmpraiz ðə hōl vəkæbjələrɪ. fɜrst, ðęr 'r ðōz wɜrdz wəð witʃ wi bɪkʌm əkwēntəd ɪn ǭrdən'rɪ kanvərsēʃn—hwɪtʃ wi lɜrn, ðæt əz tə sē, frəm ðə męmbərz əv ar ōn fæmɪlɪ ən frəm ar fəmɪljər əsōʃəts,
5 ən witʃ wi ʃəd nō ən jūz ɪvn ɪf wi kud nat rɪd ən rait. ðē kənsɜrn ðə kamən þɪŋz əv laif, ənd 'r ðə stak ɪn trēd əv ǫl u spīk ðə lęŋgwɪdʒ. sʌtʃ wɜrdz me bɪ kǫld "papjəl'r," sins ðe bəlǫŋ tə ðə pīpl ət lārdʒ ənd 'r nat ðɪ ɪksklūzɪv pəzęʃn əv ə limətəd klæs.

ǫn ðɪ ʌðər hænd, ar lęŋgwɪdʒ ɪnklūdz ə mʌltɪtūd əv wɜrdz hwɪtʃ
10 'r kəmpærətəvlɪ sęldm jūzd 'n ǭrdənərɪ kanvərsēʃn. ðęr mīnɪŋz 'r nōn tu ęvrɪ ędʒəketəd pɜrsn, bət ðər əz litl əkęʒn tu ɪmplǫi ðəm ət hōm 'r ən ðə markət-plēs. ar fɜrst əkwēntəns wəð ðəm kʌmz nat frəm ar mʌðərz lips 'r frəm ðə tǫk əv ar skūlmēts, bət frəm buks ðət wi rīd, lęktʃərz ðət wi hīr, ǫr ðə mǭr fǭrm'l kanvərsēʃn əv hailɪ ędʒəketəd
15 spīkərz, hu 'r dəskʌsɪŋ sʌm pərtikjələr tapɪk ən ə stail əprōprɪətlɪ ęləvetəd əbʌv ðɪ əbitʃuəl lęvl əv ęvrɪdē laif. sʌtʃ wɜrdz 'r kǫl "lɜrnəd," 'n ðə dəstɪŋkʃn bətwīn ðęm ən "papjəl'r" wɜrdz ɪz əv grēt əmpǭrtns tu ə rait ʌndərstęndɪŋ əv lɪŋgwistɪk prasęs.

ðə dif'rns bətwīn papjəl'r ən lɜrnəd wɜrdz me bɪ ɪzəlɪ sīn 'n ə
20 fjū əgzæmplz. wi me dəskraib ə gɜrl əz "laivlɪ" ǫr əz "vəvēʃəs." ɪn ðə fɜrst kēs, wi 'r jūzɪŋ ə nētɪv ɪŋglɪʃ fǭrm ʃn frəm ðə fəmɪljər naun "laif." ɪn ðe lætər, wi 'r jūzɪŋ ə lætn dərivətɪv hwɪtʃ həz prəsaislɪ ðə sēm mīnɪŋ. jęt ðɪ ætməsfɪr əv ðə tū wɜrdz əz kwait dif'rnt. nō wʌn ęvr gat ðɪ ædʒɪktɪv "laivlɪ" aut əv ə buk. ɪt əz ə pārt əv
25 ęvrɪbadɪz vəkæbjələrɪ. wi kænət rəmęmbər ə taim węn wi did nat nō ɪt, ən wi fīl ʃūr ðət wi lɜrnd ət lǫŋ bɪfǫr wi wər ēbəl tə rīd. ǫn ðɪ ʌðər hænd, wi mʌst əv pæst sęv'rəl jɪrz əv ar laivz bɪfǫr lɜrnɪŋ ðə wɜrd "vəvēʃəs." wi me ɪvn rəmęmbər ðə fɜrst taim wi sǫ ɪt 'n print ǫr hɜrd ət frəm sʌm grōnʌp fręnd hu wəz tǫkɪŋ ovr ar tʃaildɪʃ hędz.
30 bōþ "laivlɪ" ən "vəvēʃəs" ər gud ɪŋglɪʃ wɜrdz, bət "laivlɪ" ɪz "papjəl'r" ən "vəvēʃəs" əz "lɜrnəd."

. . . .

ęvrɪ ędʒəketəd pɜrsən hæz ət līst tū wēz əv spīkɪŋ ɪz mʌðər tʌŋ.

ðə fərst əz ðæt hwĭtʃ ĭ ĭmplǫiz ən ĭz fæmlĭ, əmʌŋ ĭz fəmiljər frę̣nz, 'nd
ǫn ǭrd'nərĭ əkēẓnz. ðə sę̣kənd əz ðæt hwĭtʃ ĭ jūzəs 'n dĭskǭrsĭŋ ǫn
35 mǭr kamplĭketəd sʌbdʒĭkts, 'nd ən ədrę̣sĭŋ pərsnz wəð hūm ĭ əz lę̣s
intəmətlĭ əkwēntəd. it əz, 'n fǭrt, ðə lę̣ŋgwĭdʒ wĭtʃ ĭ ĭmplǫiz wən ĭ
əz "ǫn ĭz dignətĭ," æz ĭ puts ǭn ĭvnĭŋ drę̣s wən ĭ ĭz gō̈ĭŋ aut tə dain.
ðə dif'rns bətwĭn ðiz tū fǭrmz əv lę̣ŋgwĭdʒ kənsists, 'n grēt mę̣ẓər,
ĭn ə dif'rns əv vəkæbjələrĭ. ðə bē̈səs əv fəmiljər wərdz məst bĭ ðə
40 sēm 'n bōþ, bət ðə vəkæbjələrĭ əprōprĭət tə ðə mǭr fǭrm'l əkēẓn wəl
ənklūd mę̣nĭ tərmz hwĭtʃ wəd bĭ stiltəd ər əfę̣ktəd ən ǭrd'nərĭ tǫk.
ðər əz ǭlso kənsid'rəbl dif'rns bətwĭn fəmiljər ən dignəfaid lę̣ŋgwĭdʒ
'n ðə mænər əv ʌtərəns. kəntræst ðə ræpəd ʌtərəns əv ar ę̣vrĭdē̈
daiəlę̣kt, ful əv kəntrækĭnz 'n klipt fǭrmz, wəð ðə mǭr dəstiŋkt
45 ənʌnsĭē̈ʃn əv ðə pulpət ər ðə plætfǭrm. ðʌs, ən kanvərsē̈ʃn, wĭ
əbitʃuəlĭ ĭmplǫi sʌtʃ kəntrækĭnz əz "ail," "dōnt," "wōnt," "its,"
"wĭd," "hĭd," 'n ðə laik, hwĭtʃ wĭ ʃəd nę̣vər jūz 'n pʌblĭk spĭkĭŋ,
ʌnlę̣s ev sę̣t pərpəs, tə giv ə mārkədlĭ kəlōkwĭəl tindʒ tə wat wĭ hæv
tə sē̈.

(Transcribed from Greenough and Kittredge's *Words and their
Ways in English Speech*, pp. 19, 20, 27, 28.)

19. Phonetic Classification of Modern English Sounds.

The vowels of Modern English are classified phonetically, according to the principles explained above in 7-14, as follows:

	BACK VOWELS		MIXED VOWELS	FRONT VOWELS
	Round	Unround	Unround	Unround
High	ū, u			ī, i, ĭ
Mid	ō, o	ā, a, ʌ	ə	ē, e, ę
Low	ǭ, ǫ		ə̄	ę̄, æ

The classification of the consonant sounds, according to the principles explained above in 1-6, is as follows:

	Velar	Palatal	Dental	Labial
Stops				
Voiced	g		d	b
Voiceless	k		t	p
Spirants				
Voiced		j	z, ẓ, ð	v
Voiceless			ʃ, s, þ	f
Nasals				
Voiced	ŋ		n	m

[l] is a "divided" consonant; it is produced by pressing the point of the tongue against the hard palate and allowing the air from the lungs to escape at the sides of the mouth; it is usually voiced, but sometimes voiceless, as in *play*.

[r] is produced by turning the point of the tongue up towards the hard palate; it is usually voiced, but sometimes voiceless, as in *try*.

[w] is a voiced, open, velar sound made with a decided rounding of the lips.

[hw] is a voiceless [w].

[h] is a breath sound made with the tongue and lips in the position, or approaching the position, which they will occupy in producing the vowel that follows.

PART II

THE LANGUAGE OF CHAUCER

PRONUNCIATION OF CHAUCER'S LANGUAGE

20. Pronunciation of Chaucer: Phonetic Notation. The following table shows the vowels and diphthongs of Chaucer's dialect of Middle English, expressed in the phonetic notation given above in section **16**, and indicates also the spellings of those sounds which are usually found in the best manuscripts of Chaucer's works.

Sound	Pronunciation			Spelling	Examples
[ā]	like a	in	father	a, aa	*bathed* [bāðəd][9b]
[a]	" o	"	fodder	a	*that* [þat]
[ē]	" a	"	mate[10]	ee, e	*swete* [swētə]
[ę̄]	" ai	"	airy	ee, e	*heeth* [hę̄þ]
[ę]	" e	"	met	e	*wende* [węndə]
[ī]	" i	"	machine[10]	i, y	*ryde* [rīdə]
[i]	" i	"	bit	i, y	*swich* [switʃ]
[ō]	" o	"	note[10]	oo, o	*roote* [rōtə]
[ǭ]	" aw	"	law	oo, o	*hooly* [hǭli]
[ǫ]	" au	"	audacious	o	*folk* [fǫlk]
[ū]	" oo	"	boot[10]	ou, ow	*fowles* [fūləs]
[u]	" u	"	full	u, o	*ful* [ful]

[9b] The brackets indicate that the spellings they enclose are phonetic spellings.

[10] The Modern English sounds given as the equivalents of Chaucer's [ē], [ī], [ō], and [ū] are only approximate equivalents, for the Modern English sounds which we have represented by the symbols [ē], [ī], [ō], and [ū] are in reality diphthongs, not simple vowels. The Modern English sounds which we have represented by [ē] and [ō] are more accurately represented phonetically by the symbols [ęe] or [ei] and [ǫo] or [ou]. The Modern English sounds that we have represented by [ī] and [ū] may be more accurately represented by the symbols [ij] and [uw]. Chaucer's [ē], [ī], [ō], and [ū] were simple vowels, pronounced like the corresponding vowels of Modern German.

[ə]	like a in about	e	*sonne* [sunnə]
[au]	" ou " out	au, aw	*faught* [fauht]
[ei̯]	" [ẹ] plus [i][11]	ai, ay, ei, ey	*day* [dẹi̯], *wey* [wẹi̯]
[eu̯]	" [ẹ] plus [u]	eu, ew	*fewe* [fẹu̯ə]
[iu̯]	" [i] plus [u][12]	u, eu, ew	*aventure* [āvẹntiu̯rə], *reule* [riu̯lə]
[oi̯]	" oy in boy	oi, oy	*coy* [kọi̯]
[ọu̯]	" [ọ] plus [u][13]	ou, ow	*bowe* [bọu̯ə]
[ou̯]	" [ǫ] plus u][14]	ou, ow, o	*foughten* [fǫu̯htən]

21. Pronunciation of Vowels, Diphthongs, and Consonants. The pronunciation of the first 117 lines of Chaucer's *Prologue* is indicated in the texts printed below on pages 14 ff. The text on the right hand pages is transcribed in the phonetic notation which has been explained above in sections 16 and 20. The text on the left hand pages is printed in the spelling of the manuscripts, but with the addition of diacritics which indicate the pronunciation of the vowels and diphthongs. The symbols which are used in the diacritical text are for the most part the same as those employed in the phonetic notation, but for greater convenience they are all given below in alphabetical order.

Symbols	Pronunciation	Examples
ā, aa	like a in father	bāthed, baar
a	" o " fodder	that
ai, ay	" ẹ plus i, approximately ey in they[15]	saide, day
au, aw	" ou in house	faught, saw
ē, ee	" a " mate	swēte, seeke
ę̄, ęę	" ai " airy	mę̄te, hęęth
ę	" e " met	węnde
ei, ey	" ẹ plus i, approximately ey in they[15]	curteis, wey

[11] A fair approximation to this sound is the a of Modern English *mate*, for this sound, as explained above in note 10, is in reality a diphthong, not a simple vowel.

[12] A fairly close approximation to this sound is the u of Modern English *mute*.

[13] If one cannot acquire this diphthong, he may substitute for it the simple vowel [ō].

[14] If one cannot acquire this diphthong, he may substitute for it the simple vowel [ǫ].

[15] See note 11 above.

Symbols	Pronunciation	Examples
eu, ew	like i in u, approximately u in mute	reule, knew
ęu, ęw	" ę " u	fęwe
ī, ȳ	" i in machine	whīl, rȳde
i, y	" i " bit	swich, lystes
ō, oo	" o " note	dōn, roote
ǭ, ǫǫ	" aw " law	ǭpen, hǫǫly
ǫ	" au " audacious	fǫlk
ǫ plus gh or h	" ǫ plus u[16]	bǫghte
ŏ	" u in full	sŏnne
oi, oy	" oy " boy	coy
ou, ow	" oo " boot	hous, fowles
ǭu, ǭw	" ǭ plus u[17]	sǭule, bǭwe
ǫu	" ǫ " u[18]	fǫughten
ü	" i " u, approximately u in mute	vęrtü
u	" u in full	ful

Unaccented e, as in sŏnne, saide, swēte, etc., is pronounced like a in Cuba. When this final e is written but is not pronounced in reading,

22.   CHAUCER IN

  Whan that Aprille with his shoures soote
  The drŏghte ǫf March hath pērced tō the roote,
  And bāthed ę̄uęry veyne in swich licour
  Ǫf which vęrtü ęngęndred is the flour;
5 Whan Zęphirus ęęk with his swēte bręęth
  Inspīred hath in ę̄uęry hǫlt and hęęth
  The tęndre crǫppes, and the yŏnge sŏnne
  Hath in the Ram his halue cours yrŏnne,
  And smāle fowles māken melōdȳe,
10 That slēpen al the nyght with ǭpen ȳe,
  Sǭ priketh hem nātüre in hir cŏrāges;
  Thannę lǭngen fǫlk tō gǭǫn ǫn pilgrimāges,
  And palmęręs fǫr tō sēken straunge strǭndes,
  Tō fęrne halwes kowthe in sŏndry lǫndes.

[16] If one cannot acquire this diphthong, he may substitute for it the simple vowel [ǫ].
[17] If one cannot acquire this diphthong, he may substitute for it the simple vowel [ǭ].
[18] This diphthong occurs only before gh or h; if one cannot acquire it, he may substitute for it the simple vowel [ǫ].

it is printed as *e* if it is **elided** before a word beginning with a vowel or "weak h"; and as ę if it is **apocopated** before a word beginning with a consonant. Unaccented e occurring between two consonants of the same word is also printed as ę when it is not pronounced in reading, that is when it is **syncopated**. For an explanation of elision, apocopation, and syncopation see section 40 below.

Chaucer's consonant sounds are in general the same as those of Modern English. It should be observed, however, that **gh** is pronounced like **ch** in German **ich, nacht**; e.g., *nyght* [niht]; initial **th** is always pronounced like **th** in **thin**; e.g., *that* [þat]; final **s** is always pronounced [s], not [z]; e.g., *was* [was], *shoures* [ʃūrəs]; **k, l,** and **w** are never silent; e.g., *knyght* [kniht], *palmers* [palmęrs], *write* [wrītə]; **ng** is pronounced like **ng** in **finger**; e.g., *yonge* [juŋgə]; **r** is strongly trilled with the tip of the tongue; consonants that are doubled in writing are usually pronounced double, as in Modern English **pen-knife**; e.g., *sonne* [sunnə], *alle* [allə].

The letters **u** and **v** were interchangeable in Chaucer's time. For example in the text printed below the letter **u** represents the sound of [v] in *euery* (line 3), and the letter **v** represents the vowel [u] in *Vnder* (line 105).

PHONETIC NOTATION[19]

hwan þat āpril wiþ is ʃūrəs sōtə
þə druht of martʃ haþ pērsəd tō þə rōtə,
and bāðəd ęvri vein in switʃ likūr
of hwitʃ vęrtiu ęndʒęndrəd is þə flūr;
5 hwan zęfirus ęk wiþ is swētə brę̄þ
inspīrəd haþ in ęvri holt and hę̄þ
þə tęndər kroppəs, and þə juŋgə sunnə
haþ in þə ram is halvə kūrs irunnə,
and smālə fūləs mākən męlōdīə,
10 þat slēpən al þə niht wiþ ǭpən īə,
sǭ prikəþ hęm nātiur in hir kurādʒəs;
þan lǭŋgən folk tō gǭn on pilgrimādʒəs,
and palmęrs for tō sēkən straundʒə strǭndəs,
tō fęrnə halwəs, kūð in sundri lǭndəs.

---

[19] The *text* used is that of Liddell, *The Prologue to the Canterbury Tales*, etc., with some changes of punctuation. All other passages quoted from Chaucer's works follow the text of Skeat's *Student's Chaucer*.

* th in function words like "that", "the" etc. is [ð]

15 And spęcially from ęuęry shīres ęnde
    Of Ęngelǫnd tō Caunturbury they węnde,
    The hǫoly blisful martir fǫr tō sēke
    That hęm hath hǫlpen whan that they wērę seeke.
        Bifil that in that sęson ǫn a day,
20 In Southwęrk at the Tabard as I lay
    Rędy tō węnden ǫn mȳ pilgrymāge
    Tō Cauntęrbury with ful dēuout cŏrāge,
    At nyght was come in tō that hǫstęlrȳe
    Wēl nȳne and twenty in a cŏmpaignȳe
25 Of sŏndry fǫlk, bȳ āuęntūre y-falle
    In felawęshipe, and pilgrimęs wērę they alle,
    That tōward Cauntęrbury wŏlden rȳde.
    The chāmbres and the stābles wēren wȳde,
    And wēl wē wēren ęsed atte bęste.
30 And shǫrtly, whan the sŏnne was tō ręste,
    Sǫ hadde I spǭken with hęm ęuęrychǭn
    That I was of hir felawęshipe anǭn,
    And māde fǫrward ęrly fǫr tō rȳse
    Tō tāke oure wey thęr as I yow dēuȳse.
35   But nāthelęēs, whīl I hauę tȳme and spāce,
    Ęer that I ferther in this tāle pāce,
    Mē thynketh it acǫrdaunt tō ręsoun
    Tō tęlle yow al the cǫndicioun
    Of ęch of hęm sǫ as it sēmed mē,
40 And whichę they wēre, and of what dēgree,
    And ęēk in what array that they wēre inne;
    And at a Knyght than wǒl I first bigynne.
        A Knyght thęr was and that a wǒrthy man,
    That frǭ the tȳme that hē first bigan
45 Tō rīden out hē lǒued chiualrīe,
    Trǫuthe and hǫnour, frēdǒm and curteisīe.
    Ful wǒrthy was hē in his lǒrdes węrre,
    And thęrtō hadde hē riden, nō man ferre,
    As wēl in cristendǒm as in hęthenęsse,

```
15      and spesiali frǫm ẹ̄vri ʃīrəs ẹndə
        ǫf ẹŋgəlǫnd tō kaunturbri þei wẹndə,
        þə hǭli blisful martir fǫr tō sēkə
        þat hem haþ hǫlpən hwan þat þei wẹr sēkə.
           bifil þat in þat sēzūn ǫn a·dẹi,
20      in sūðwẹrk at þə tabard as I lẹi
        rẹdi tō wẹndən ǫn mī pilgrimādʒə
        tō kauntẹrbri wiþ ful dēvūt kurādʒə,
        at niht was kum in tō þat ǫstẹlrīə
        wēl nīn and twẹnti in a kumpẹinīə
25      ǫf sundri fǫlk, bī āvẹntiur ifallə
        in felauʃip, and pilgrims wẹr þei allə,
        þat tōward kauntẹrburi wǭldən rīdə.
        þə tʃāmbərs and þə stābəls wẹrən wīdə,
        and wēl wē wẹrən ẹ̄zəd attə bẹstə.
30      and ʃǫrtli, hwan þə sunnə was tō rẹstə,
        sǭ had I spǭkən wiþ ẹm ẹ̄vritʃǭn
        þat I was ǫf hir felauʃip anǭn,
        and mādə fǫrward ẹ̄rli fǫr tō rīzə
        tō tāk ūr wẹi þẹr as I jū dēvīzə.
35         but nāðəlẹ̄s, hwīl I av tīm and spāsə,
        ẹ̄r þat I fẹrðər in þis tālə pāsə,
        mē þiŋkəþ it akǫrdaunt tō rẹ̄zūn
        tō tellə jū al þə kǫndisiūn
        ǫf ẹ̄tʃ ǫf hem sǭ as it sēməd mē,
40      and hwitʃ þei wẹrə, and ǫf hwat dēgrē,
        and ẹ̄k in hwat arrẹi þat þei wẹr innə;
        and at a kniht þan wul I first biginnə.
           a kniht þẹr was and þat a wurði man,
        þat frǭ þə tīmə þat ē first bigan
45      tō rīdən ūt hē luvəd tʃivalrīə,
        trǭuð and ǫnūr, frēdǭm and kurtẹizīə.
        ful wurði was ē in is lǫrdəs wẹrrə,
        and þẹrtō had ē ridən, nǭ man fẹrrə,
        as wēl in kristəndǭm as in hẹ̄ðənẹssə,
```

50 And ẹvẹre honoured for his wŏrthynẹsse.
    At Alisaundre hē was whan it was wŏnne;
    Ful ofte tymẹ hē haddẹ the bǫrd bigǒnne
    Abǒuen alle nacions in Prūce.
    In Lẹttǫw hadde hē reysed and in Rūce,
55 Nǫ cristen man sǫ ofte of his dēgree.
    In Gernade at the seege ẹẹk haddẹ hē bē
    Of Algẹzir and riden in Bẹlmarȳe.
    At Lȳeys was hē and at Satalȳe
    Whan they wẹrẹ wŏnne, and in the Grẹte Sẹẹ.
60 At many a nǫble armee haddẹ hē bē.
    At mortal batailles haddẹ hē been fiftēne,
    And foughten for ourẹ feith at Tramyssēne
    In lystes thrīes, and ay slayn his foo.
    This ilke wŏrthy knyght haddẹ been alsǫ
65 Sǒmtȳme with the lǫrd of Palatȳe
    Agayn anōther hẹthen in Turkȳe;
    And ẹuerẹmǫǫrẹ hē haddẹ a sǒuẹreyn prȳs.
    And though that hē wẹrẹ wŏrthy, hē was wȳs,
    And of his port as meekẹ as is a mayde.
70 Hē nẹuerẹ yẹt nǫ vileynȳẹ ne sayde
    In al his lȳf vntǒ nǫ manẹr wight.
    Hē was a vẹrray parfit, gẹntil knyght.
    But for tǒ tẹllen yow of his array,
    His hors wẹrẹ goode, but hē was nat gay;
75 Of fustian hē wẹred a gypon
    Al bismōterẹd with his habẹrgeon,
    For hē was lāte y-comẹ from his viāge
    And wẹnte for tǒ doon his pilgrymāge.
         With hym thẹr was his sǒnẹ, a yŏng Squīēr,
80 A lǒuyẹre and a lusty bachẹlēr,
    With lokkes crulle, as they wẹrẹ leyd in prẹsse.
    Of twẹnty yẹẹr of āge hē was, I gẹsse;
    Of his statūrẹ hē was of ẹuẹne lẹngthe
    And wŏnderly dēlyuẹre and of grẹẹt strẹngthe;

50 and ęvr onūrəd fqr is wurðinęssə.
at alisaundr ē was hwan it was wunnə;
ful oftə tīm hē had þə bǫrd bigunnə
abuvən allə nāsiūns in priusə.
in lętǫu had ē ręizəd and in riusə,
55 nǫ kristən man sǫ oft of his dēgrē.
in gęrnād at þə sēdʒ ęk had ē bē
of aldʒęzīr and ridən in bęlmarīə;
at līęis was ē and at satalīə
hwan þęi węr wun, and in þə grętə sę̄.
60 at mani a nǫbəl armē had ē bē.
at mǫrtal batęils had ē bēn fiftēnə,
and fouhtən for ūr fęiþ at tramisēnə
in listəs þrīəs, and ęi slęin is fǫ.
þis ilkə wurði kniht had bēn alsǫ
65 sumtīmə wiþ þə lǫrd of palatīə
agęin anōðər hęðən in turkīə;
and ęvərmǫr hē had a suvręin prīs.
and þouh þat hē węr wurði, hē was wīs,
and of is pǫrt as mēk as is a męidə.
70 hē nęvər jęt nǫ vilęinī nə sęidə
in al is līf untō nǫ manęr wiht.
hē was a vęrręi parfit, dʒęntil kniht.
but for tō tęllən jū of his arręi,
his hors węr gōdə, but ē was nat gęi;
75 of fustian hē węrəd a dʒipūn
al bismutərd wiþ is habęrdʒūn,
for hē was lāt ikum from his vīādʒə
and węntə for tō dōn is pilgrimādʒə.
      wiþ im þęr was is sun, a jung skwīęr,
80 a luvjęr and a lusti batʃęlēr,
wiþ lokkəs krul, as þęi węr lęid in pręssə.
of twęnti jęr of ādʒ ē was, ī gęssə;
of his statiur hē was of ęvnə lęŋgþə
and wundərli dēlivr and of grēt stręŋgþə;

85   And hē haddę been sŏmtymę in chyuachīe
     In Flaundrēs, in Artoys, and Pycardīe,
     And bǭrn hym weel, as ǫf sǭ lītel spāce,
     In hǭpę tǒ stǫnden in his lādy grāce.
     Ęmbrouded was hē, as it wę̄re a mę̄ede
90   Al ful ǫf fręsshe floures whȳte and rę̄ede;
     Syngyngę hē was ǫr floytyngę al the day;
     Hē was as fręssh as is the mōnthę of May.
     Shǫrt was his gownę, with slēues lǭngę and wȳde;
     Wēl koudę hē sittę ǫn hǫrs and faire rȳde;
95   Hē koudę sǫngēs māke and wēl ęndīte,
     Iustę and ę̄ek dauncę, and weel purtreyę and wrīte.
     Sǭ hǫǫtę hē lŏued that bȳ nyghtertāle
     Hē sleep namǫǫrę than dooth a nyghtyngāle.
     Curteis hē was, lǭwęly and sęruysāble,
100 And carf bifǭrn his fader at the tāble.
          A Yēman haddę hē and sęruantz namǭ
     At that tȳmę, fǫr hym liste rīde sǫǫ,
     And hē was clad in cǭtę and hood ǫf grēne.
     A shę̄ef ǫf pę̄cǫk arwes, bright and kēne,
105 Vnder his bęlt hē bār ful thriftilȳ—
     Wēl koudę hē dręssę his takel yēmanlȳ,
     His arwes drouped nǫght with fętherēs lǭwe—
     And in his hand hē baar a myghty bǭwe.
     A nǫt hę̄ed haddę hē, with a broun visāge;
110 Ǫf woodecraft wēl koudę hē al the v̈sāge.
     Vpǫn his arm hē baar a gay brācēr
     And bȳ his sȳde a swērd and a bŏkęlēr,
     And ǫn that oother sȳdę a gay daggēre
     Harneised wēl and sharp as point ǫf spę̄re;
115 A Cristǫphrę on his brēst ǫf siluer sheene,
     An hǭrn hē bār, the bawdryk was ǫf grēne;
     A forster was hē soothly, as I gęsse.

85 and hē had bēn sumtīm in tʃivatʃīə
    in flaundərs, in artǫis, and pikardīə,
    and bǭrn im wēl, as ǫf sǭ lītəl spāsə,
    in hǭp tō stǭndən in is lādi grāsə.
    ęmbrūdəd was ē, as it węr a mędə
90 al ful ǫf fręʃə flūrəs hwīt and rędə;
    siŋgiŋg ē was ǫr flǫitiŋg al þə dęi;
    hē was as fręʃ as is þə mōnþ ǫf męi.
    ʃǫrt was is gūn, wiþ slēvəs lǭŋg and wīdə;
    wēl kūd ē sit ǫn hǫrs and fęirə rīdə;
95 hē kūdə sǭŋgəs māk and wēl ęndītə,
    dʒust and ęk dauns, and wēl purtręi and wrītə.
    sǭ hǫt hē luvəd þat bī nihtərtālə
    hē slēp namǭr þan dōþ a nihtiŋgālə.
    kurtęis ē was, lǭuli and sęrvizābəl,
100 and karf bifǭrn is fader at þə tābəl.

       a jēman had ē and sęrvants namǭ
    at þat tīm, fǫr im listə rīdə sǭ,
    and hē was klad in kǫt and hōd ǫf grēnə.
    a ʃęf ǫf pękǫk arwəs, briht and kēnə,
105 undər is bęlt ē bār ful þriftilī—
    wēl kūd ē dręs is takəl jēmanlī,
    his arwəs drūpəd nǫuht wiþ fęðrəs lǭuə—
    and in is hand ē bār a mihti bǭuə.
    a nǫt hę̄d had ē wiþ a brūn vizādʒə;
110 ǫf wōdəkraft wēl kūd ē al þə iuzādʒə.
    upǫn is arm hē bār a gęi brāsēr
    and bī is sīd a swērd and a buklēr,
    and ǫn þat ōðər sīd a gęi dagērə
    harnęizəd wēl and ʃarp as pǫint ǫf spērə;
115 a kristǫfr ǫn is bręst ǫf silvər ʃēnə,
    an hǭrn ē bār, þə baudrik was ǫf grēnə;
    a fǫrstər was ē sōþli, as I gęssə.

23. Relation of Sounds to Spelling. The spelling of the vowels and diphthongs in the manuscripts of Chaucer's works is far from phonetic. In a phonetic system of spelling each character represents one sound, and only one. In the manuscripts of Chaucer, however,

a	represents	[ā] or [a]
e	"	[ē], [ę̄], or [ę]
ee	"	[ē] or [ę̄]
i	"	[ī] or [i]
o	"	[ō], [ǭ], [ǫ], [u], or [ǫu]
oo	"	[ō] or [ǭ]
ou	"	[ū], [ǭu], or [ǫu]
u	"	[u] or [iu]
y	"	[ī] or [i]

But in spite of these ambiguities of spelling, the pronunciation of a word in Chaucer's dialect can usually be inferred from the pronunciation of the word in Modern English.

a	represents [ā]	if in MnE the vowel is			[ē]; ME nāme, MnE [nēm]
a	"	[a]	" " " "	"	[æ]; ME that, MnE [ðæt]
ee or e	"	[ē] or [ę̄]	" " " "	"	[i]; ME swēte, hęęth; MnE [swīt], [hīþ]
e	"	[ę]	" " " "	"	[ę]; ME węnde, MnE [węnd]
i or y	"	[ī]	" " " "	"	[ai]; ME rȳde, MnE [raid]
i or y	"	[i]	" " " "	"	[i]; ME riden, MnE [ridən]
oo or o	"	[ō]	" " " "	"	[ū]; ME rōte, MnE [rūt]
oo or o	"	[ǭ]	" " " "	"	[ō]; ME hǫǫly, MnE [hōlī]
o	"	[ǫ]	" " " "	"	[a]; ME ǫxe, MnE [aks][20]
o	"	[u]	" " " "	"	[ʌ]; ME sǒne, MnE [sʌn]
o	"	[ǫu]	" " " "	"	[ǭ]; ME thoght, MnE [þǭt]
ou or ow	"	[ū]	" " " "	"	[au]; ME hous, MnE [haus]
ou or ow	"	[ǭu]	" " " "	"	[ō]; ME bǫwe, MnE [bō]
ou	"	[ǫu]	" " " "	"	[ǭ]; ME foughte, MnE [fǭt]
u	"	[u]	" " " "	"	[ʌ]; ME under, MnE [ʌndər]
u	"	[iu]	" " " "	"	[jū] or [ū]; ME hūmour, rūde; MnE [hjūmər], [rūd]

[20] In the dialect of most parts of the United States, ME [ǫ] has become [a], but the ME vowel (or a vowel much like it) has been retained in the speech of England and New England.

24. The basis of the statements just made is that tho the pronunciation of the English vowel sounds has changed greatly since Chaucer's time, it has changed in a systematic and consistent way. Middle English [ǭ] has regularly developed into Modern English [ō]; [hǭil] has become [hōli], [bǭt] has become [bōt], [ǭpən] has become [ōpən], [sǭ] has become [sō]. That is, under the same conditions, a given Middle English sound has always developed into a certain corresponding Modern English sound.

But the conditions are *not* always the same. The development of a sound is often affected by the influence of other sounds which precede or follow it. Thus, Middle English [u] regularly developed into Modern English [ʌ]; [sunnə] has become [sʌn], [undər] has become [ʌndər], [luvə] has become [lʌv]. But when Middle English [u] was preceded by a lip consonant (**b**, **p**, **f**, or **w**) and was followed by **l**, it has been preserved in Modern English; e.g., Middle English [bulə], [pullə], [ful], and [wulf] are Modern English [bul], [pul], [ful], and [wulf]. Moreover, vowels change not only in quality, but also in quantity. Long vowels may become short, and short vowels may become long. For example, in a number of words Middle English [ō], which has regularly become [ū] in Modern English, is represented by Modern English [u]. This is not because Middle English [ō] has in these words changed to [u] instead of [ū], but because, after [ō] had become [ū], the [ū] was shortened to [u]. Thus we have Modern English [gud], [hud], and [stud] from Middle English **gōd**, **hōd**, and **stōd**. So also with Modern English [breþ] from Middle English **brēth**; Middle English [ę̄] regularly changed to Modern English [ī], but in this case [ę̄] was shortened to [ę] before the change to [ī] occurred.

25. The statements, therefore, that have been made with regard to the relation between Middle English sounds and Modern English sounds are not sufficient to enable us to determine the pronunciation of *all* Middle English words. But where the evidence of the Modern English pronunciation is not clear, it is almost always possible to determine the Middle English pronunciation of a *native* English word from a knowledge of its pronunciation in Old English.[21]

---

[21] Likewise, the pronunciation of ME words that were borrowed from French can be determined from a knowledge of their pronunciation in Old French; the Modern French pronunciation of such words is often different.

a	represents [ā]	if in OE the vowel was a or æ in an open syllable;[22] OE nama, fæder; ME nāme, fāder
a	"	[a] if in OE the vowel was a or æ in a closed syllable;[23a] OE þanc, þæt; ME thank, that
ee or e	"	[ē] if in OE the vowel was ē or ēo; OE swēte, bēon; ME swēte, been
ee or e	"	[ę̄] if in OE the vowel was ēa, or e in an open syllable; OE ēac, mete; ME ę̄k, mę̄te
e	"	[ę] if in OE the vowel was e or eo in a closed syllable; OE helpan, weorc; ME hęlpen, węrk
i or y	"	[ī] if in OE the vowel was ī or ȳ; OE rīdan, fȳr; ME rīden, fȳr
i or y	"	[i] if in OE the vowel was i or y; OE drincan, fyllan; ME drinken, fillen
oo or o	"	[ō] if in OE the vowel was ō; OE dōn; ME dōn
oo or o	"	[ǭ] if in OE the vowel was ā, or o in an open syllable; OE hālig, stolen; ME hǭly, stǭlen
o	"	[ǫ] if in OE the vowel was o in a closed syllable; OE oxa; ME ǫxe
o	"	[u] if in OE the vowel was u; OE sunu; ME sŭne
ou	"	[ū] if in OE the vowel was ū; OE hūs; ME hous
u	"	[u] if in OE the vowel was u; OE under; ME under

By the application of the rules that have been given in this section of the grammar the student will be able to ascertain the pronunciation of the great majority of the words that occur in Chaucer's works. A more systematic and detailed account of the history of English sounds will be found in sections 42-45 below.

---

[22] An open syllable is one that ends in a vowel; in words of two or more syllables a single consonant following a vowel belongs to the following syllable; so in OE nama, fæder, mete, and stolen, a, æ, e, and o were in open syllables.

[23a] A closed syllable is one that ends in a consonant; examples of vowels in closed syllables are a, æ, e, and o in OE þanc, þæt, helpan, and oxa. Every vowel which is followed by two or more consonants is in a closed syllable.

INFLECTIONS OF CHAUCER'S LANGUAGE

26. Declension of Nouns. The regular inflection of nouns in Chaucer, as exemplified by **dom**, *judgment*, and **ende**, *end*, is as follows:

Sing. Nom., Dat., Acc.	dom	ende
Gen.	domes	endes
Plur. Nom., Gen., Dat., Acc.	domes	endes

The following exceptions occur:

1. The genitive singular of proper nouns ending in **s** is frequently without ending; e.g., *Epicurus owne sone*, A 336.
2. The genitive singular of nouns of relationship ending in **r** is sometimes without ending; e.g., *my fader soule*, A 781; *brother sone*, A 3084.[23b]
3. The genitive singular of nouns which belonged to the Old English "weak" declension is sometimes without ending; e.g., *his lady grace*, A 88; *the sonne up-riste*, A 1051.[24]
4. The plural sometimes ends in **s** instead of **es**; e.g., *naciouns*, A 53; *hunters*, A 178; *fees*, A 317; this is particularly common in words of one syllable ending in a vowel and in words of two or more syllables ending in a consonant. The ending -es is often written when only **s** is sounded; e.g., *yeddinges*, A 237.
5. The plural of some nouns ends in **en** instead of **es**; e.g., *eyen*, A 152; *children*, A 1193.[25]
6. The plural of monosyllabic nouns ending in **s** is usually without ending; e.g., *caas*, A 323.

[23b] These nouns had no ending in the genitive singular in Old English.

[24] The Old English genitive singulars of Chaucer's **lady** and **sonne** were **hlǣfdigan** and **sunnan**, which in early Middle English became **ladie(n)** and **sunne(n)**, the **n** in parenthesis being a sound which was very often lost. The genitive singulars **lady** and **sonne** in Chaucer are the early Middle English forms without **n**, the three syllables of early Middle English **ladie** having been contracted to two.

[25] Some of these nouns, such as **eyen**, from Old English **ēage**, belonged in Old English to the weak declension, which had the ending -an in the nominative and accusative plural. Others, such as **children**, from Old English **čild**, plural **čildru**, did not belong in Old English to the weak declension but assumed the weak ending -en in Middle English from the analogy of nouns which had been weak in Old English.

7. Some nouns which had no ending in the nominative and accusative plural in Old English have no plural ending in Chaucer; e.g., *hors*, A 74; *swyn*, A 598; *yeer*, A 82.[26]

8. The dative singular has the same form as the nominative-accusative singular, but in certain phrases consisting of a preposition immediately followed by a noun the noun has the old dative ending -e; e.g., *of towne*, A 566.[27]

27. **Declension of Adjecitves.** In Middle English, as in Modern German, there are two declensions of the adjective, the strong and the weak. The weak declension of the adjective is used when it is preceded by the definite article **the**, by a demonstrative (**this** or **that**), by a possessive pronoun, or by a noun in the genitive case; e.g., *the yonge sonne*, A 7; *this ilke monk*, A 175; *his halfe cours*, A 8; *Epicurus ownes one*, A 336; the weak declension is also used when the adjective precedes a noun used in direct address; e.g., *faire fresshe May*, A 1511; it may also be used when the adjective precedes a proper name not used in direct address; e.g., *faire Venus*, A 2663.

The forms of the strong and weak declensions of the adjectives **good** and **swete** are as follows:

Strong Declension			
	Singular	**good**	**swete**
	Plural	**goode**	**swete**
Weak Declension			
	Singular	**goode**	**swete**
	Plural	**goode**	**swete**

It will be observed that (1) adjectives like **swete** are invariable in form; (2) adjectives like **good** have in the strong declension the ending -e in the plural; (3) adjectives like **good** have in the weak declension the ending -e in both singular and plural.

The following exceptions occur:

1. Plural adjectives used predicatively are often not inflected, tho such adjectives are frequently written with a final e even when the e is not sounded; e.g., *whiche they weren*, A 40; *And of another thing they were as fayn*, A 2707.

---

[26] These were neuter nouns in Old English.
[27] See note 33 below.

2. Adjectives of two or more syllables ending in a consonant are usually not inflected, either in the plural or in the circumstances which call for the use of the weak inflection; e.g., *mortal batailles*, A 61; *He which that hath the shortest shal biginne*, A 836.

3. A trace of the old genitive plural of the adjective **all** appears occasionally in the form **aller, alder-** (from Old English **ealra**, genitive plural of **eal**); e.g., *hir aller cappe*, "the cap of them all," A 586; *alderbest*, "best of all," A 710.

28. Personal Pronouns The personal pronouns are inflected as follows in Chaucer; forms that are rare are placed in parentheses.

1. First and second persons:

Sing. Nom.	I, (ich)	thou
Gen.	my, myn	thy, thyn
Dat., Acc.	me	the
Plur. Nom.	we	ye
Gen.	our, oure, (oure)	your [jŭr], youre, (youre)
Dat., Acc.	us	you [jū]

2. Third person:

Sing. Nom.	he	she	hit, it
Gen.	his	hir, hire, (hire); her, here, (here)	his
Dat., Acc.	hym	hir, hire, (hire); her, here, (here)	hit, it
Plur. Nom.		they	
Gen.		hir, hire, (hire); her, here, (here)	
Dat., Acc.		hem	

29. Demonstratives. The demonstratives **this** and **that** are inflected as follows in Chaucer; forms that are rare are placed in parentheses.

Sing.	this	that
Plur.	this, thise, (thise); thes, these, (these)	tho [bọ̄]

A trace of the old dative singular of **that** appears in the phrase *for the nones*, A 379, from Old English *for þæm ānes* (literally "for that once"); the early Middle English form of this phrase was *for then ones*, which by incorrect word division, came to be written in Chaucer's time *for* *the nones*. A survival of the old instrumental case of **that** appears in the adverbial **the** (Old English þē); e.g., *the more merry*, A 802, literally "more merry by that."

30. Strong and Weak Verbs. In Middle English, as in Old English and all other Germanic languages, there are two conjugations of verbs, the strong and the weak. Weak verbs form their preterit by means of a suffix containing **d** or **t**. Strong verbs form their preterit by means of a change in the vowel of the stem of the verb. For example, the preterits of the weak verb **loven** and the strong verb **riden** are as follows:

Pret. Ind. Sing.	1	lovede, loved	rood
	2	lovedest	ride
	3	lovede, loved	rood
Plur.		lovede(n)[28], loved	ride(n)

Weak verbs may be recognized from the fact that their preterit indicative first and third persons singular ends in **-ede**, **-ed**, **-de**, or **-te** and from the fact that their past participle ends in **-ed**, **d**, or **t**. Strong verbs may be recognized from the fact that their preterit indicative first and third persons singular is **without ending**, and from the fact that their past participle ends in **-en** or **e**.

31. Endings of Weak Verbs. There are two types of weak verbs in Middle English. Weak verbs of Type I have preterits ending in **-ede** or **-ed** and past participles ending in **-ed**. Weak verbs of Type II have preterits ending in **-de** or **-te** and past participles ending in **-ed**, **d**, or **t**. The principal parts of representative verbs are as follows:

Type I	love(n)	lovede, lovedę, loved	loved
	were(n)	werede, weredę, wered	wered
Type II	here(n)	herde	hered
	fele(n)	felte	feled
	fede(n)	fedde	fed
	seke(n)	soughte	sought

The endings of the weak verbs, exemplified by **love(n)** of Type I and **here(n)** of Type II, are as follows:

Pres. Ind. Sing.	1 lov-e	her-e
	2 lov-est	her-est

[28] **e(n)** indicates that the ending **-en** interchanges with the ending **-e**.

	3	lov-eth	her-eth
Plur.		lov-e(n)	her-e(n)
Pret. Ind. Sing.	1	lov-ede, lov-edę, lov-ed	her-de
	2	lov-edest	her-dest
	3	lov-ede, lov-edę, lov-ed	her-de
Plur.		lov-ede(n), lov-edę, lov-ed	her-de(n)
Pres. Subj. Sing.		lov-e	her-e
Plur.		lov-e(n)	her-e(n)
Pret. Subj. Sing.		lov-ede, lov-edę, lov-ed	her-de
Plur.		lov-ede(n), lov-edę, lov-ed	her-de(n)
Imperative Sing.		lov-e	her
Plur.		lov-eth	her-eth
Infinitive		lov-e(n)	her-e(n)
Gerund		to lov-e(n)	to her-e(n)
Pres. Participle		lov-ingę, lov-ingę, lov-ing	her-ingę, her-ingę, her-ing
Past Participle		lov-ed	her-ed

32. Endings of Strong Verbs. Strong verbs form their preterit by means of a change in the vowel of the stem of the verb. The vowel of the preterit plural is often different from that of the preterit singular, so that there are four principal parts, the infinitive, the preterit indicative first person singular, the preterit indicative plural, and the past participle.[29] The principal parts of representative strong verbs are as follows:

ride(n) [rīdən]	rood [rǭd]	ride(n) [rīdən]	ride(n) [rīdən]
crepe(n) [krēpən]	creep [krēp]	crope(n) [krǭpən]	crope(n) [krǭpən]
binde(n) [bīndən]	bond [bǭnd]	bounde(n) [būndən]	bounde(n) [būndən]
helpe(n) [hęlpən]	halp [halp]	holpe(n) [hǫlpən]	holpe(n) [hǫlpən]
sterve(n) [stęrvən]	starf [starf]	storve(n) [stǫrvən]	storve(n) [stǫrvən]
bere(n) [bęrən]	bar [bar]	bere(n) [bērən]	bore(n) [bǭrən]
	baar [bār]	bare(n) [bārən]	
	beer [bēr]		
speke(n) [spękən]	spak [spak]	speke(n) [spękən]	spoke(n) [spǭkən]
		spake(n) [spākən]	

[29] The vowel of the infinitive occurs also in the present indicative, present subjunctive, imperative, gerund, and present participle; the vowel of the preterit indicative first person singular occurs also in the preterit indicative third person singular; the vowel of the preterit indicative plural occurs also in the preterit indicative second person singular and in the preterit subjunctive; the vowel of the past participle occurs in that form only.

shake(n) [ʃākən]   shook [ʃōk]   shooke(n) [ʃōkən]   shake(n) [ʃākən]
slepe(n) [slēpən]   sleep [slēp]   slepe(n) [slēpən]   slēpe(n) [slēpən]
holde(n) [hǭldən]   heeld [hēld]   heelde(n) [hēldən]   holde(n) [hǭldən]

The endings of the strong verbs, exemplified by ride(n) and bere(n), are as follows:

Pres. Ind. Sing. 1	rid-e	ber-e
2	rid-est	ber-est
3	rid-eth, rit [rit][30]	ber-eth
Plur.	rid-e(n)	ber-e(n)
Pret. Ind. Sing. 1	rood	bar
2	rid-e, rood	ber-e, bar
3	rood	bar
Plur.	rid-e(n)	ber-e(n)
Pres. Subj. Sing.	rid-e	ber-e
Plur.	rid-e(n)	ber-e(n)
Pret. Subj. Sing.	rid-e	ber-e
Plur.	rid-e(n)	ber-e(n)
Imperative Sing.	rid	ber
Plur.	rid-eth	ber-eth
Infinitive	rid-e(n)	ber-e(n)
Gerund	to rid-e(n)	to ber-e(n)
Pres. Participle	rid-inge, rid-ingę, rid-ing	ber-inge, ber-ingę, ber-ing
Past Participle	rid-e(n)	bor-e(n)

33. Preteritive-Present Verbs. The preteritive-present (or strong-weak) verbs have **present** indicatives which are like the **preterit** indicatives of strong verbs in that they have no ending in the first and third persons singular. The **preterits** of these verbs are **weak**. The principal forms of the more important preteritive-present verbs that occur in Chaucer are as follows:

Pres. Ind. Sing. 1	can, *be able, know how*	dar, *dare*
2	canst	darst
3	can	dar
Plur.	conne(n) [kunnən], can	dorre(n) [durrən], dar

[30] Contracted forms like rit are frequent in verbs whose stems end in d or t; the contraction originated in Old English.

INFLECTIONS OF CHAUCER'S LANGUAGE

Pret. Ind. Sing. 1 kouthe [kūðə], koude [kūdə]   dorste [durstə]
Pres. Ind. Sing. 1 **may**, *be able*   **moot**, *be permitted, be under obligation*
          2 **mayst**   most
          3 **may**   moot
      Plur.   **mowe(n)** [mūwən], **may**   mote(n), moot
Pret. Ind. Sing. 1 **mighte**   moste
Pres. Ind. Sing. 1 **shal**, *be about to, be under obligation*   wot [wǫt], *know*
          2 **shalt**   wost [wǫst]
          3 **shal**   wot
      Plur.   **shulle(n), shul, shal**   wite(n), wot
Pret. Ind. Sing. 1 **sholde** [ſuldə], [ſǭldə]; **shulde**   wiste

34. Anomalous Verbs. The forms of **bee(n)**, *be*, are as follows:

     Pres. Ind. Sing. 1 **am**
                  2 **art**
                  3 **is**
           Plur.   **bee(n), be**
     Pret. Ind. Sing. 1 **was**
                  2 **were**
                  3 **was**
           Plur.   **were(n)**
     Pres. Subj. Sing. **be**
           Plur.   **bee(n), be**
     Pret. Subj. Sing. **were**
           Plur.   **were(n)**
     Imperative Sing. **be**
           Plur.   **beeth**
     Infinitive   **bee(n), be**
     Gerund   **to bee(n), to be**
     Pres. Participle   **being**
     Past Participle   **bee(n), be**

The forms of **wille(n)**, *will*, are as follows:

     Pres. Ind. Sing. 1 **wil, wol** [wul]
                  2 **wilt, wolt**

       3 **wil, wol**
     Plur. **wille(n), wolle(n), wil, wol**
Pret. Ind. Sing. 1 **wolde** [wǭldə], [wuldə]
       2 **woldest**
       3 **wolde**
     Plur. **wolde(n)**
Pret. Subj. Sing. **wolde**
     Plur. **wolde(n)**
Infinitive   **wille(n)**
Past Participle **wold**

FINAL e IN CHAUCER'S LANGUAGE

35. Inflectional and Etymological Final e. Final e in Chaucer's language is either **inflectional** or **etymological**. Inflectional final e's are those which occur in some forms of a word but not in others; their occurrence or non-occurrence depending on grammatical considerations. For example, the adjective **good** has no final e in such an expression as *A good man was ther of religioun* (A 477), but it has a final e in the ex- expressions *His hors were gode* (A 74) and *his gode name* (A 3049). In A 74 **gode** has a final e because it is a **plural** adjective, in A 3049 it has a final e because it is a **weak** adjective (see 27 above); but in A 477 **good** is without final e because it is neither plural nor weak. On the other hand, the adjective **lene** has a final e in the expression *As lene was his hors as is a rake* (A 287) tho it is neither plural nor weak. The explanation of the final e in **lene** is not grammatical but etymological; the word has a final e because it ended in e in Old English, being derived from Old English **hlǣne**. Final e in **goode** is inflectional, final e in **lene** is etymological.

36. Inflectional Final e. Inflectional final e occurs in adjectives and verbs.

 1. Adjectives (see 27 above)
  Final e occurs:
   a. In the weak form of the adjective
   b. In the plural form of the adjective[21].

---

[21] When it modifies a plural noun the pronoun **his** is very commonly written **hise** in good manuscripts, and the final e is sometimes pronounced. This final e is from the analogy of the final e of plural adjectives. So also is the final e of **these, thise**, plural of **thes, this** (see 29 above).

2. Verbs (see 31-33 above)

Final e occurs:

    a. In the present indicative first person singular of **strong** and **weak** verbs

    b. In the preterit indicative first and third persons singular of **weak** verbs

    c. In the preterit indicative second person singular of **strong** verbs

    d. In the present subjunctive singular of **strong** and **weak** verbs

    e. In the preterit subjunctive singular of **strong** and **weak** verbs

    f. In the imperative singular of many **weak** verbs

    g. In the gerund of **monosyllabic** verbs, e.g., **to done**, F 334

    h. In the present participle of **strong** and **weak** verbs

Final e interchanging with en occurs:

    i. In the present indicative plural of **strong** and **weak** verbs

    j. In the preterit indicative plural of **strong** and **weak** verbs

    k. In the present subjunctive plural of **strong** and **weak** verbs

    l. In the preterit subjunctive plural of **strong** and **weak** verbs

    m. In the infinitive and gerund of **strong** and **weak** verbs

    n. In the past participle of **strong** verbs[32]

37. **Etymological Final e.** Etymological final e occurs in nouns, adjectives, pronouns, adverbs, prepositions, and conjunctions.

1. Nouns

Final e occurs:

    a. In nouns derived from Old English nouns which ended in a vowel (**a**, **e**, or **u**); e.g., **tyme**, from OE **tima** (A 44); **sonne**, from OE **sunne** (A 7); **tale**, from OE **talu** (A 36)

    b. In nouns derived from Old English **feminine** nouns which ended in a consonant; e.g., **reste**, from OE **rest**, fem. (A 30)

    c. In some nouns derived from Old English nouns ending in **-en**; e.g., **mayde**, from OE **mægden** (A 69)

    d. In nouns derived from Old French nouns ending in e; e.g., **corage**, from OFr **corage** (A 22)

---

[32] For simplicity the preteritive-present verbs, are ignored in this paragraph. Their preterits are like those of weak verbs, and their present indicative plural either has the ending -e(n) or is without ending. (See 33 above.)

e. In the "petrified" dative which occurs in certain phrases consisting of a preposition immediately followed by a noun; e.g., **out of towne** (A 566)[33]

2. Adjectives

   Final **e** occurs:

   a. In adjectives derived from Old English adjectives ending in **e**; e.g., **lene**, from OE **hlǣne** (A 287)

   b. In the comparative form of a few adjectives; e.g., **more**, from OE **māra, māre**[34]

   c. In the "petrified" dative which occurs in certain phrases consisting of a preposition immediately followed by an adjective used as a noun; e.g., **with-alle** (A 127)

   d. In adjectives derived from Old French adjectives ending in **e**; e.g., **straunge**, from OFr **estrange** (A 13)

3. Pronouns

   Final **e** is usually written and occasionally pronounced in **oure**, from OE **ūre**; in **hire, here** (*her*), from OE **hire**; and in **hire, here** (*their*) from OE **hira, heora**

4. Adverbs, Prepositions, and Conjunctions

   Final **e** occurs:

   a. In adverbs derived from adjectives; e.g., **faire** (A 94), from the adjective **fair** (A 154)

   b. In adverbs, prepositions, and conjunctions whose originals had a final vowel in Old English; e.g., **sone**, from OE **sōna** (B 1702); **thanne**, from OE **þonne** (D 2004); **inne**, from OE **inne** (A 41); **whanne**, from OE **hwonne** (F 1406)

   c. In adverbs, prepositions, and conjunctions whose originals in Old English ended in -an; e.g., **bifore**, from OE **beforan** (A 377); **with-oute**, from OE **wiþūtan** (A 343); **sithe**, from OE **siþþan**

---

[33] The final **e** in **of towne** is not a genuine inflection in the English of Chaucer's time. In early Middle English the dative singular always ended in e, but in the course of time the accusative was substituted for the dative wherever the two cases differed in form. A few phrases, however, like **of towne, on live, to bedde**, etc., were in such constant use that they resisted change and were preserved unaltered long after the dative form had become obsolete in the language as a whole. We find therefore that Chaucer says **of towne** in A 566, but **of the toun** in A 217.

[34] The usual comparative ending is -er.

38. Inorganic Final e. A few nouns and adjectives in Middle English had final e's (not inflectional) which cannot be explained upon any of the grounds stated in **37**; e.g., **gate** (C 729), from OE ǧeat, neut.; **dale** (B 4013), from OE dæl, neut.; **weye** (B 385), from OE weǧ, masc.; **pere** (F 678), from OFr per; **bare** (A 683), from OE bær; **harde** (D 2228), from OE heard. Such final e's we call **inorganic** final e's. These words acquired final **e** in early Middle English as the result of some analogy or association which in most cases we are not able to trace with certainty.

39. Scribal e's. Occasionally even in the best and earliest manuscripts of Chaucer, and frequently in the poorer and later manuscripts, final e's are written which were never pronounced in Middle English. Such e's we call **scribal** e's. An example is **month** (A 92), from OE mōnaþ, masc.; the word is written with final **e** in the Ellesmere manuscript, but is never pronounced with final **e** in Chaucer or in the language of any other Middle English writer.

40. Elision, Apocope, and Syncope. If one pronounces in reading Chaucer's verse all the final e's that are grammatically or etymologically justifiable, the metrical structure of the verse is often seriously impaired or entirely destroyed. It is clear that Chaucer did not intend that every possible final **e** should be sounded. Final **e** is usually **elided** when the following word begins with a vowel or "weak **h**";[35] e.g., in **couthe** (A 14) and **dresse** (A 106). Moreover, final **e** is often lost before words beginning with a consonant; e.g., **wiste** (A 224), **tyme** (A 102), **mete** (A 136). The loss of final **e** before consonants is called **apocope** or **apocopation**. This is to be distinguished from **syncope** or **syncopation**, which is the loss of a vowel **between** two consonants of the same word; e.g., "*Cometh neer,*" *quod he,* "*my lady prioresse*" (A 839). In using apocopated forms in his verse, however, Chaucer was not doing violence to the language of his time, as a modern writer would be doing if he omitted the final vowel of *navy* or *china*. In Chaucer's time the final **e** was beginning to be lost, and by the end of the fifteenth century it had entirely disappeared from the language. In Chaucer's time the final **e** was still pronounced, but not universally, so that forms both with and without final **e** were in use. Chaucer, therefore, tho he generally preferred the forms with final **e**, used the forms without final **e** when it suited him to do so. He always used the forms with final **e** in rime.

[35] "Weak **h**" is the **h** in words like **he, him, hem, her, hath, hadde**, etc., in which the **h** was pronounced only when the word was strongly stressed, and the silent **h** in French words like **honour**, etc.

PART III

THE HISTORY OF ENGLISH SOUNDS

40. Pronunciation of Old English. The pronunciation of the Old English vowels and diphthongs is shown in the following table:

OE Spelling	Pronunciation	Examples
ā	[ā]	stān, *stone* [stān]
a	[a]	man, *man* [man]
ǣ	[ę̄]	hǣþ, *heath* [hę̄þ]
æ	[æ]	þæt, *that* [þæt]
ē	[ē]	swēte, *sweet* [swētę]
e	[ę]	helpan, *help* [hęlpan]
ī	[ī]	rīdan, *ride* [rīdan]
i	[i]	drincan, *drink* [driŋkan]
ō	[ō]	dōn, *do* [dōn]
o	[ǫ]	crop, *crop* [krǫp]
ū	[ū]	hūs, *house* [hūs]
u	[u]	sunu, *son* [sunu]
ȳ	[ȳ]	fȳr, *fire* [fȳr]
y	[y]	þynne, *thin* [þynnę]
ēa	[ę̄ə]	strēam, *stream* [strę̄əm]
ea	[æə]	hearpe, *harp* [hæərpę]
ēo	[ēo]	bēon, *be* [bēon]
eo	[ęo]	weorc, *work* [węork]
īe	[īə]	hīeran, *hear* [hīəran]
ie	[iə]	ieldra, *elder* [iəldra]

The pronunciation of the Old English consonants is shown in the following table:

OE Spelling	Pronunciation	Examples
c	[k]	cēpan, *keep* [kēpan]
ċ	[tʃ]	ċīdan, *chide* [tʃīdan]

OE Spelling	Pronunciation	Examples
cg	[dz]	brycg, *bridge* [brydz]
g	[ɣ]	boga, *bow* [boɣa]
ġ	[j]	ġiefan, *give* [jiəvan]
ng	[ŋg]	singan, *sing* [siŋgan]
sc	[ʃ]	scip, *ship* [ʃip]

h before consonants and after vowels is pronounced like **ch** in German **ich, nacht**; e.g., niht, *night*, hēah, *high*.

f and **s** are pronounced like [v] and [z] when they occur between vowels, as in ġiefan, *give*, and rīsan, *rise*; like [f] and [s] when they are initial or final, as in fæder, *father*, stæf, *staff*, sunu, *son*, wæs, *was*.

þ and **ð** are used without distinction for the sounds [þ] and [ð]. They are pronounced like [ð] when they occur between vowels, as in cūðe, *knew*; like [þ] when they are initial or final, as in þæt, *that*, cūþ, *known*.

r is strongly trilled with the tip of the tongue.

The other Old English consonants are pronounced as in Modern English. But double consonants were pronounced double, as in Modern English *pen-knife, book-case*.

41. Old English in Phonetic Notation. The Old English version of the parable of the Good Samaritan, Luke 10:30-35, in the Old English spelling and accompanied by a literal translation, is as follows:

Sum   man fērde fram Hierusalem tō Hiericho and becōm on
A-certain man went from Jerusalem to Jericho and fell among

þā scaðan, þā hine berēafodon and tintregodon hine and forlēton
the thieves, who him robbed and tortured him and left

hine samcwicne. þā ġebyrede hit þæt sum sācerd fērde on
him half-alive. Then happened it that a-certain priest went on

þām ilcan weġe; and þā hē þæt ġeseah, hē hine forbēah.
the same way; and when he that saw, he from-him turned-away.

And eall swā sē dīacon, þā hē wæs wið þā stōwe and þæt ġeseah,
And all so the deacon, when he was by the place and that saw,

hē hine ēac forbēah. þā fērde sum Samaritanisc
he from-him also turned-away. Then went a-certain Samaritan

man wið hine; þā hē hine ġeseah, ðā wearð hē mid
man opposite him; when he him saw, then became he with

mildheortnesse ofer hine āstyred. þā   ġenēalǣhte hē and wrāð
pity   over him moved. Then   approached he and bound

his wunda and on āġēat ele and wīn and hine on his nīeten sette
his wounds and in poured oil and wine and him on his beast set

and ġelǣdde on his lǣċehūs and hine lācnode; and brōhte ōþrum
and took into his hospital and him treated; and brought the-next

dæġe twēġen peningas and sealde þām lǣċe and þus cwæð,
day two pennies and gave to-the physician and thus said,

"Beġīem his; and swā hwæt swā þū māre tō ġedēst,
"Take-care-of him; and whatever thou more in-addition doest,

þonne iċ cume, iċ hit forġielde þē."
when I come, I it shall-repay thee."

Transcribed in phonetic notation the Old English passage just given is
as follows:

sum man fērdę fram hiəruzalęm tō hiəriko and bękōm on þā ſaðan, þā
hinę bęrę̄əvodon and tintręgodon hinę and forlēton hinę samkwiknę.
þā jębyrędę hit þæt sum sākęrd fērdę on þām ilkan węję; and þā hē þæt
jęsææh, hē hinę forbę̄əh. and æəll swā sē dīakon, þā hē wæs wiþ þā
stōwę and þæt jęsææh, hē hinę ę̄ək forbę̄əh. þā fērdę sum samaritaniſ
man wiþ hinę; þā hē hinę jęsææh, þā wæərþ hē mid mildhęortnęssę over
hinę āstyręd. þā jęnę̄əlę̄htę hē and wrāþ his wunda and on āję̄ət ęlę
and wīn and hinę on his nīətęn sęttę and jęlę̄ddę on his lętſęhūs and hinę
lāknodę; and brōhtę ōðrum dæję twējęn pęnıngas and sæəldę þām lętſę
and þus kwæþ, "bęjīəm his; and swā hwæt swā þū mārę tō jędēst,
þonnę itſ kumę, itſ hit forjiəldę þē."

42. Normal Development of Old English Vowels. The normal development[26] of the Old English vowel sounds in the Midland dialect of Middle English and of the Middle English sounds in Modern English is shown in the following table:

---

[26] The normal development of a vowel is that which took place when its development was not affected by the influence of neighboring sounds or by changes of quantity. An account of the changes that took place in the English vowel sounds as a result of these special conditions will be found below in sections 43 and 44.

NORMAL DEVELOPMENT OF OLD ENGLISH VOWELS

	Old English[37]			Middle English			Modern English	
ā	[ā]	stān	[stān]	[ǭ]	ston	[stǭn]	[ō][39c]	[stōn]
a	[a]	þanc	[þaŋk]	[a]	thank	[þaŋk]	[æ]	[bæŋk]
æ	[æ]	þæt	[þæt]	[a]	that	[þat]	[æ]	[ðæt]
ǣ	[ḗ]	hǣþ	[hḗþ]	[ḗ]	heeth	[hḗþ]	[ī][39c]	[hīþ]
ē	[ē][38]	swēte	[swēte]	[ē][38]	swete	[swētə]	[ī][39c]	[swīt]
e	[ę]	helpan	[hęlpan]	[ę]	helpe(n)	[hęlpən]	[ę]	[hęlp]
ī	[ī][38]	rīdan	[rīdan]	[ī][38]	ride(n)	[rīdən]	[ai]	[raid]
i	[i]	drincan	[driŋkan]	[i]	drinke(n)	[driŋkən]	[i]	[driŋk]
ō	[ō][38]	fōda	[fōda]	[ō][38]	fode	[fōdə]	[ū][39c]	[fūd]
o	[ǫ]	oxa	[ǫksa]	[ǫ]	oxe	[ǫksə]	[a][39d]	[aks]
ū	[ū][38]	hūs	[hūs]	[ū][38]	hous	[hūs]	[au]	[haus]
u	[u]	sunu	[sunu]	[u]	sone	[sunə]	[ʌ]	[sʌn]
ȳ	[ȳ]	fȳr	[fȳr]	[ī]	fyr	[fīr]	[ai]	[fair]
y	[y]	fyllan	[fyllan]	[i]	fille(n)	[fillən]	[i]	[fil]
ēa	[ḗə]	strēam	[strḗəm]	[ḗ]	streem	[strḗm]	[ī][39c]	[strīm]
ea	[æə]	earm	[æərm]	[a]	arm	[arm][39b]		
ēo	[ḗo]	bēon	[bḗon]	[ē][39a]	bee(n)	[bēn]	[ī][39c]	[bī]
eo	[ęo]	weorc	[węork]	[ę][39a]	werk	[węrk][39b]		

[37] The Old English sounds which are taken as the basis of this table are those of the **Mercian** dialect, which was that from which the Midland dialect of Middle English was derived. The sounds of the **Mercian** dialect differed in certain respects from those of West-Saxon, which is the dialect in which most of the Old English literature is preserved and upon which the Old English dictionaries are based. For example, the Mercian dialect did not contain the West-Saxon diphthongs īe and ie, and it had the vowel ē in many words which in West-Saxon have the vowel ǣ; e.g., West-Saxon dǣd was Mercian dēd. In the Mercian dialect the vowel ǣ was always the result of umlaut.

[38] The Modern English sounds given as the equivalents of Old and Middle English ē, ī, ō, and ū are only approximate equivalents, for (as explained above in note 10) the Modern English sounds which we have represented by the symbols [ē], [ī], [ō], and [ū] are in reality diphthongs, not simple vowels. Old and Middle English ē, ī, ō, and ū were simple vowels, pronounced like the corresponding vowels of Modern German.

[39a] It is probable that OE ēo and eo first changed (at least in some localities) to early ME [ȫ] and [ö], and that [ȫ] and [ö] developed later into [ē] and [e]. The symbols [ȫ] and [ö] represent respectively the vowels of German hören and wörter.

[39b] The Modern English development of the vowel in this word is due to the that follows it; see 44, 1 below.

[39c] The Modern English sounds which we represent by the symbols [ē] [ī], [ō] and [ū] are in reality, as explained above in notes 33 and 10, diphthongs, not simple vowels.

[39d] ME [ǫ], or a vowel much like it, has been preserved in the speech of England and New England, but it has become [a] in most parts of the United States.

The following table shows the normal development in Modern English of certain sounds which developed in Middle English as the result of certain special conditions which will be explained below in section 43.

Middle English			Modern English	
[ā]	name	[nāmə]	[ē][10]	[nēm]
[au]	faught	[fauht]	[ǭ]	[fǭt]
[ei]	they	[þei]	[ē][40]	[ðē]
[eu]	fewe	[feuə]	[jū]	[fjū]
[iu]	humour	[hiumūr], rude [riudə]	[jū] or [ū]	[hjūmər], [rūd]
[oi]	boy	[boi]	[oi]	[boi]
[ǭu]	bowe	[bǭuə]	[ō][40]	[bō]
[ou]	thoght	[þouht]	[ǭ]	[þǭt]

43. Special Developments in Middle English. The most important special developments of the Old English vowel sounds in Middle English are as follows:

1. Changes in the quantity of vowels.

   a. Shortening of long vowels. Old English long vowels were shortened in early Middle English (before the end of the twelfth century) when they were followed by a double consonant or by a group of two or more consonants;[41] e.g., OE lǣdde, ME ledde [leddə]; OE lǣssa, ME lesse [lessə]; OE cēpte, ME kepte [keptə]; OE wīsdōm, ME wisdom [wisdōm].

   Old English long vowels were also frequently shortened in Middle English when the second syllable of the word was [ī]; e.g., OE ǣniġ, ME eny [enī]; OE sāriġ, ME sory [sorī].

[40] The Modern English sounds which we represent by the symbols ē and ō are in reality, as explained above in notes 38 and 10, diphthongs, not simple vowels.

[41] Shortening of long vowels did not take place, however, before the consonant groups (see note 42 below) which caused lengthening in late Old English. Nor did it take place before the combination st unless a third consonant followed; it is for this reason that we have MnE [kraist] from Old English Crīst, but MnE [krisməs] from Old English crīstmæsse.

b. **Lengthening of short vowels.**[42] In the thirteenth century the short vowels a, e, and o were lengthened in open syllables,[43a] so that a became [ā],[43b] e became [ẹ̄], and ǫ became [ǭ]; e.g., OE **nama**, ME **name** [nāmə]; OE **fæder**, ME **fader** [fādər]; OE **mete**, ME **mete** [mẹ̄tə]; OE **stolen**, ME **stolen** [stǭlən]. This lengthening did not take place, however, when the second syllable of the word was [i]; e.g., OE **hefiġ**, ME **hevy** [hęvi]; OE **bodiġ**, ME **body** [bǫdī]. And we often find short a, e, and o in open syllables when the second syllable of the word ended in l, r, m, or n; e.g., OE **sadol**, ME **sadel** [sadəl]; OE **wæter**, ME **water** [watər]; OE **heofon**, ME **heven** [hęvən].

2. **Development of new diphthongs.**

As may be seen from the table of sound changes given above in section 42, the Old English diphthongs ēa, ea, ēo, and eo became simple vowels in Middle English. In Middle English, however, there developed a new series of diphthongs: [ai], [ęi], [au], [ęu], [iu], [ǫi], [ǭu], and [ǫu]. The principal sources of these diphthongs in the Midland dialect were as follows:

[ai] developed out of Old English æ followed by [j], spelled ġ; e.g., OE **dæġ** [dæj], ME **dai**; OE **sæġde** [sæjdę], ME **saide**. In early Middle English this diphthong had the sound of [ai], but in late Middle English it became identical in sound with the diphthong [ęi].

---

[42] In late Old English all short vowels were lengthened when they were followed by one of the consonant combinations ld, mb, nd, ng, rd, rn, and rð. Many long vowels which originated in this way remained long thruout the Middle English period and have developed in Modern English like the other Middle English long vowels; e.g., OE **feld**, ME **feeld** [fēld], MnE [fīld]; OE **findan**, ME **finde(n)** [fīnden], MnE [faind]; OE **grund**, ME **ground** [grūnd], MnE [graund]. Modern English [ōld] is from Middle English [ǭld], which developed regularly from late Old English **āld**, earlier **ald** (West-Saxon **eald**). But in a great many words these lengthened vowels were shortened in Middle English. Shortening always occurred when the consonant group was followed by a third consonant; e.g., OE **ċild**, MnE [tʃaild] from ME [tʃīld], but MnE [tʃildrən] from ME [tʃildrən].

[43] For a definition of open syllable see note 22 above.

[43b] Previous to the period when short vowels were lengthened in open syllables, Old English **ā** had become [ǭ] in Middle English, and for a certain period, therefore, the sound [ā] did not exist in the language. But when a was lengthened in open syllables the sound [ā] was reintroduced. The [ā] which originated in this way never became [ǭ].

[ei] developed out of Old English e, ē or ǣ, followed by [j], spelled ġ; e.g., OE weġ [wej], ME wey [wei]; OE twēġen [twējen], ME tweie(n); OE ǣġ [ēj], ME ei [ei].

[au] developed:

(1) out of Old English a followed by w; e.g., OE clawu [klawu], ME clawe [klauə];

(2) out of Old English a followed by [ɣ], spelled g;[44] e.g., OE dragan [draɣan], ME drawe(n) [drauən];

(3) out of Old English ea followed by h; e.g., OE feaht, ME faught [fauht].

[eu] developed out of Old English ēa followed by w; e.g., OE fēawe [fēəwə], ME fewe [feuə].

[iu] developed out of Old English ī followed by w; e.g., OE stīweard [stiwæərd], ME stiward [stiuard]. But the commonest source of [iu] in Middle English was the French vowel [ȳ], which was written u. The sound [ȳ] did not occur in the Midland dialect of Middle English, and therefore French loan-words which contained this sound were pronounced with the diphthong [iu], which was the nearest English equivalent; e.g. ME nature [nātiurə], from Old French nature [natȳrə].[45]

[oi] occurs almost exclusively in French loan words; e.g., ME joie from Old French joie.

[ọu] developed:

(1) out of Old English ā or ō followed by w; e.g., OE cnāwan [knāwan], Middle English knowe(n) [knọuən]; OE grōwan [grōwan], ME growe(n) [grọuən].

---

[44] This sound, the g of North German sagen, is not a stop consonant (like g in go) but an open consonant or spirant which somewhat resembles English w but is made without any rounding of the lips.

[45] A diphthong spelled ew also developed out of OE ēo followed by w, e.g., in ME knew from OE cnēow. Some scholars are of opinion that this diphthong had the sound of [eu] or [ēu]. It no doubt had this sound in very early ME, but it seems probable that in Chaucer's time it had become [iu]. This may be inferred from the fact that French loan words which had [ȳ] in Old French are very frequently spelled in Middle English with ew instead of u, e.g., vertew, crewel, instead of vertu, cruel, and also from the fact that the [iu] which developed in ME out of OE īw was also spelled ew or u instead of īw or iu, e.g., steward and Tuesday (from OE Tīwes dæġ).

(2) out of Old English ā followed by [ȝ], spelled g; e.g., OE āgen [āȝen], ME owe(n) [ǭuən].

(3) out of Old English o when it was in an open syllable followed by [ȝ]; e.g., OE boga [boȝa], ME bowe [bǭuə].

[ǫu] developed out of Old English o, ō, or ā followed by ht; e.g., OE bohte, ME boughte [bǫuhtə]; OE sōhte, ME soghte [sǫuhtə]; OE āhte, ME oughte [ǫuhtə].[46]

44. Special Developments in Modern English. The normal development of the Middle English vowel sounds in Modern English has been shown above in section 42. The most important special developments that took place as the result of the influence of neighboring sounds or changes of quantity are these:

1. Special developments before r

Middle English [e] followed by r often changed to [a] in late Middle English or very early Modern English and later developed into [ā]; e.g., ME sterve(n) [stervən], early MnE [starv], MnE [stārv].

Middle English [a] followed by r has become [ā] in Modern English; e.g., ME hard [hard], MnE [hārd].

Middle English [ǫ] followed by r has become [ǭ] in Modern English; e.g., ME for [fǫr], MnE [fǭr].

Middle English [ir] and [ur] have regularly, and Middle English [er] has frequently, become [ɔ̄r] in Modern English; e.g., ME first [first], MnE [fɔ̄rst]; ME curse(n) [kursən], MnE [kɔ̄rs]; ME lerned [lernəd], MnE [lɔ̄rnəd].

Middle English [ā] and [ei] followed by r have become Modern English [ē]; ME spare(n) [spārən], MnE [spēr]; ME fair [feir], MnE [fēr].

Middle English [ẹ̄] has frequently been preserved before r in Modern English; e.g., ME bere(n) [bẹ̄rən], MnE [bẹ̄r].

Modern English [ī] and [ū] before r, for example in [hīr] and [fūr] are not the [ī] and [ū] of [īt] and [būt], but a little more open; in quality they approximate to lengthened [i] and [u].

---

[46] The ō of OE sōhte was shortened before ht (see 43, 1a above); the ā of OE āhte first became [ǭ] and was then shortened to [ǫ] before the ht.

Middle English [ō] and [ǭ] followed by r have become [ǭ] in Modern English; e.g., ME swoor [swōr], MnE [swǭr], ME more [mǭrə], MnE [mǭr].⁴⁷

2. Special developments before l.

Middle English [a] followed by l plus another consonant or final l was diphthongised to [au] in early Modern English; this diphthong then developed, like Middle English [au], into [ǭ]; e.g., ME smal [smal], early MnE [smaul], MnE [smǭl]; ME bald [bald], early MnE [bauld], MnE [bǭld].⁴⁸

Middle English [ǫ] followed by l was diphthongised to [ǭu] in early Modern English; this diphthong then developed, like Middle English [ǭu], into Modern English [ō]; e.g., ME folk [fǫlk], early MnE [fǭulk], MnE [fōk].

3. Special developments after [w].

When preceded by w Middle English [a] (including the [a] which developed from [ę] before r) became [ǫ] in the seventeenth century and has since developed into Modern English [ǭ] or [a]; e.g., ME water [watər], MnE [wǭtr]; ME warm [warm], MnE [wǭrm]; ME washen [wašən], MnE [wašˇ].⁴⁹

4. Development of Modern English [ã].

In standard British English and in the dialect of southern New England, Middle English [a] has developed with more or less regularity into [ã] when followed by

lm,	e.g.,	MnE	[kãm]
lf,	"	"	[kãf]
lv,	"	"	[sãv]
[š], final	"	"	[tšãš]

---

⁴⁷ Long vowels before r in Modern English are really diphthongs to a greater or less degree; e.g., starve, for, fair, hear, and sure are rather [staərv], [fǫər], [fęər], [hiər], and [tuər] than [stãrv], [fǫr], [fęr], [hir], and [tãr].

⁴⁸ But before lm, lf, and lv Middle English [a] has developed into [ã] or [ę̃]; see 44, 4 below.

⁴⁹ British standard English has [ǫ] for American [a] in these words, but both in England and America there is a good deal of fluctuation between [ǭ] and [ǫ] or [a].

[ð],	e.g.,	MnE	[fāðər]
[þ],	”	”	[păþ]
[ft],	”	”	[āftər]
[s], final	”	”	[glās]
st,	”	”	[pāst]
sk,	”	”	[āsk]
sp,	”	”	[klāsp]
[sf],	”	”	[blāsfīm]
mp,	”	”	[ęgzāmpl]
nt,	”	”	[tšānt]
nd,	”	”	[kəmānd]
[ns]	”	”	[dāns]
[ntʃ],	”	”	[stāntʃ]

In American English the great majority of these words have the vowel [æ] or [ę̄], e.g., [pæþ], [pę̄þ]; [æsk], [ę̄sk], etc.

5. Preservation of Middle English [ū] and [u].

Middle English [ū] has been preserved in Modern English before lip consonants (b, p, m, f, v); e.g., ME stoupe(n) [stūpən], MnE [stūp]; ME toumbe [tūmbə], MnE [tūm]. In some words this [ū] before lip consonants was shortened to [u] and afterwards changed to [ʌ]; e.g., ME shouve(n) [šūvən], MnE [ʃʌv]; ME double [dūbəl], MnE [dʌbl]; ME roum [rūm], MnE [rum], also [rūm].

Middle English [u] has been preserved in Modern English under the following circumstances: regularly between lip consonants and l; e.g., ME bole [bulə], MnE [bul]; ME ful [ful], MnE [ful]; ME wolf [wulf], MnE [wulf]; and frequently between lip consonants and consonants other than l; e.g., ME wode [wudə], MnE [wud]; ME putte(n) [puttən], MnE [put].

6. [ū] for Middle English [iu].

Middle English [iu] has become [ū] under the following circumstances: regularly after r, and after l preceded by another consonant; e.g., ME rude [riudə], MnE [rūd]; ME blew [bliu], MnE [blū]; and frequently after l, s, t, d, and n; e.g., ME lute [liutə], MnE [lūt]; ME Susanne [siuzannə], MnE [sūzən]; ME Tuesday [tiuəsdęi], MnE (especially American) [tūzdī]; ME due [diuə], MnE (especially American) [dū]; ME newe [niuə], MnE (especially American) [nū].

7. [i] for Middle English [ẹ].

Middle English [ẹ] has become [i] when followed by n plus another consonant or combination of consonants (not [þ] or [tʃ], e.g., MnE **strength, bench**); e.g., ME **Engelond** [ęngəlǭnd], MnE [iŋglənd].

8. Shortening of Middle English [ẹ̄].

Before Middle English [ẹ̄] had become [ī] it was often shortened in Modern English when it was followed by d, t, or [þ]; e.g., ME **deed** [dẹ̄d], MnE [dęd]; ME **swete(n)** [swẹ̄tən], MnE [swęt]; ME **deeth** [dẹ̄þ], MnE [dęþ].

9. Shortening of [ū] from Middle English [ō].

After Middle English [ō] had become [ū], the [ū] was in a great many words shortened when it was followed by d, t, or k; in some words the result of this shortening is [u], but in others the [u] has undergone the further change of [u] to [ʌ]; e.g., ME **good** [gōd], MnE [gud]; ME **blood** [blōd], MnE [blʌd]; ME **foot** [fōt], MnE [fut]; ME **book** [bōk], MnE [buk].

10. Lengthening of [i] before [h].

When [h] in the combination **ht** was lost, a preceding [i] was lengthened to [ī] and was afterwards changed to [ai]; e.g., ME **right** [riht], MnE [rait].

11. Lengthening of Middle English [ǫ] and [a].

Middle English [ǫ] has frequently been lengthened in Modern English to [ǭ] when followed by [f], [s], or [þ]; e.g., ME **of** [ǫf], MnE [ǭf]; ME **los** [lǫs], MnE [lǭs]; ME **motthe** [mǫþþə], MnE [mǭþ].

In American English, Middle English [ǫ] has commonly been lengthened to [ǭ] when followed by [ŋg]; e.g., ME **long** [lǫŋg], MnE [lǭŋ]; it is also often lengthened when followed by [g]; e.g., ME **frogge** [frǫggə], MnE [frǭg], also [frag] and (in New England) [frǫg].

In American English, Modern English [æ] from Middle English [a] has commonly been lengthened to [ę̄] when followed by d, [g], m, n, ng; e.g., ME **glad** [glad], MnE [glę̄d], ME **land** [land], MnE [lę̄nd]; ME **sang** [saŋg], MnE [sę̄ŋ].

45. Vowels in Unaccented Syllables. The sound changes which have been explained in the preceding sections are those which were undergone by vowels in accented syllables. The changes which were undergone in Middle English by the Old English vowels of unaccented syllables are very much simpler in their character, and will be considered later in connection with the inflections of Middle English.[50]

46. Consonant Sounds. The most important changes that have taken place in the consonant sounds of English are these:

1. Middle English changes.

Old English final **m** in unstressed syllables became Middle English **n**; e.g., OE **endum**, ME **enden**.

Final **n** was very frequently lost in unstressed syllables, so that the common inflectional ending **-en** was very often reduced to **-e**; e.g., OE **singan**, ME **singen** or **singe**.

Old English initial **hn, wl, hl,** and **hr** became Middle English **n, l, l,** and **r**; e.g., OE **hnecca**, ME **necke**; OE **wlispian**, ME **lispen**; OE **hlāf** ME **lof**; OE **hring**, ME **ring**.

Old English initial [ȝ], which was an open consonant or spirant, became in Middle English the stop consonant [g];[51] e.g., OE **gōd** [ȝōd], ME **good** [gōd]. But when it was preceded by a consonant and followed by a vowel, Old English [ȝ] became [w]; e.g., OE **hālgian**, ME **halwie(n)**.

2. Modern English changes.

Initial [þ] changed to [ð] in a number of pronouns and particles which were commonly pronounced without stress, e.g., **the, they, them, thou, thee, thy, that, those, this, these, then, than, there**.

Final [f], [s], and [þ] became [v], [z], and [ð] if they were preceded by a vowel that was without stress or if they occurred in words that were commonly pronounced without stress in the sentence; e.g., ME **actif**, MnE **active**; ME **of** [ǫf], MnE [əv];[52] ME **faces** [fāsəs], MnE [fēsəz]; ME **his** [his], MnE [hiz]; ME **with** [wiþ], MnE [wið].

---

[50] See section 48 below.

[51] When it was not initial but was preceded by a vowel, [ȝ] lost its consonantal quality and united with the vowel to form a diphthong; see section 43, 2 above.

[52] Modern English **off** [ǭf] is the stressed form of **of**; in **of** the [f] changed to [v] because of lack of stress, but in **off** the [f] remained unchanged.

Initial **gn** and **kn** have become **n** and initial **wr** has become **r**; e.g., ME **gnawe(n)** [gnauən], MnE [nọ̄]; ME **knight** [kniht], MnE [nait]; ME **write(n)** [wrītən], MnE [rait].

Final **mb** has been reduced to **m**; e.g., ME **domb** [dumb], MnE [dʌm].

Final [ŋg] has been reduced to [ŋ]; e.g., ME **thing** [þiŋg], MnE [þiŋ].

l has been lost before **k** and the lip consonants **m** and **f** when the vowel that preceded it was Middle English [a] or [ǫ]; e.g., ME **talke(n)** [talkən], MnE [tọ̄k]; ME **folk** [fǫlk], MnE [fōk]; ME **palm** [palm], MnE [pām]; ME **half** [half], MnE [hāf].

[h] has been lost before consonants and after vowels; e.g., ME **night** [niht], MnE [nait]; ME **saugh** [sauh], MnE [sọ̄].[53]

Middle English double consonants have become single in Modern English; e.g., ME **sonne** [sunnə], MnE [sʌn]; ME **sitte(n)** [sittən], MnE [sit].

[sj] and zj] have become [ʃ] and [ʒ]; e.g., early MnE **special** [spɛsjal], MnE [spɛʃl]; early MnE **mission** [misjon], MnE [miʃən]; early MnE **portion** [pǫrsjon], MnE [pǫrʃən];[54] early MnE **vision** [vizjon], MnE [viʒən].

[tj] and [dj] have become [tʃ] and [dʒ]; e.g., early MnE **fortune** [fǫrtjun], MnE [fǫrtʃən]; early MnE **cordial** [kǫrdjæl], MnE [kǫrdʒl].

r in Modern English has lost its trilled sound and has become a vowel-like sound which tends to disappear before consonants.

---

[53] In some words Middle English [h] has become [f] in Modern English; e.g., ME **laughe(n)** [lauhən], MnE [lāf]; ME **tough** [tūh], MnE [tʌf]; in these words the vowel has also been modified in a special way; in the examples just given ME [au] has become [ā] instead of [ǭ], and ME [ū] has been shortened to [ʌ].

[54] The suffix -tion is merely a Latinised spelling of the suffix which was spelled **-cioun** or **-cion** in Middle English.

PART IV

HISTORICAL DEVELOPMENT OF MIDDLE ENGLISH INFLECTIONS

47. Declension of Nouns. The declension of nouns in Old English was rather complex; there were four cases, nominative, genitive, dative, and accusative; two numbers, singular and plural; and three genders, masculine, feminine, and neuter, which, like those of modern German, were largely independent of sex. In the late Middle English of Chaucer, on the other hand, the declension of nouns is extremely simple. The simplification which took place in the inflection of nouns in Middle English was the result of two causes, sound change and analogy.

48. Sound Change in Unaccented Syllables. The Middle English sound changes that were undergone by vowels in accented syllables have been explained in sections 42 and 43. The changes undergone by vowels in unaccented syllables were very much simpler in character and may be briefly stated as follows:

Old English a, e, o, and u became in unaccented syllables the vowel which was commonly written e and which probably was pronounced [ə];[55] e.g.

OE belle [bellɛ]   ME belle [bellə]
OE oxa [ǫksa]   ME oxe [ǫksə]
OE nacod [nakǫd]   ME naked [nākəd]
OE sunu [sunu]   ME sune [sunə]

This change in the pronunciation of vowels of unaccented syllables is the most important difference between Old English and Middle English.

---

[55] This unstressed vowel was also frequently written i, particularly in the North of England; it is probable that this variation of spelling represents a variation of pronunciation between [ə] and [ɪ].

49. Analogy. Analogy is the regularising, simplifying tendency of the human mind manifesting itself in language. The child who says *mans* for *men*, *foots* for *feet*, and *fighted* for *fought* is making use of analogy. In Modern English the preterits *dreamed* and *lighted* have been substituted for the older forms *dreamt* and *lit* because of the analogy of the great number of weak verbs which have the same vowel in the preterit as in the present. So in the Middle English noun declensions, many forms which were merely the Old English forms pronounced in a new way were displaced by different forms that were suggested by analogy. For example, in Old English and early Middle English the dative singular and the accusative singular were identical in the great majority of nouns. But in some nouns the dative singular ended in **e** and the accusative singular ended in a consonant. In these nouns, therefore, the analogy of the other nouns caused the old dative singular to be superseded by a form which was identical with the accusative. The Middle English forms that were developed from the Old English forms by sound change alone are called **historical** forms. Forms that were substituted for these historical forms by the process of analogy are called **analogical** forms.

NOUNS

50. Development of the Middle English Noun Declensions. The development of the Middle English noun declensions is shown in the tables printed below. In the first column are given the Old English forms. In the second column are given the **historical** Middle English forms that developed from the Old English forms by the process of sound change alone. In the third column are given **analogical** forms that displaced some of the historical forms. In the fourth column are given the late Middle English forms which we find (for example) in Chaucer; in this column the historical forms are printed in Roman type and the analogical forms in italics. The words in the first column exemplify the eleven principal types of noun declension in Old English: the strong masculine nouns **dōm** (*judgment*) and **ende** (*end*); the u-declension noun **sunu** (*son*); the strong feminine nouns **lufu** (*love*) and **hwīl** (*time*); the strong neuter nouns **lim** (*limb*), **hors** (*horse*), and **wīte** (*punishment*); the weak masculine noun **hunta** (*hunter*); the weak feminine noun **sunne** (*sun*); and the weak neuter noun **ēare** (*ear*).

NOUNS

	OLD ENGLISH	MIDDLE ENGLISH		
		Historical forms	Analogical forms	Late ME

51. dōm, masculine:

Sing. Nom.	dōm	doom		doom
Gen.	dōmes	doomes		doomes
Dat.	dōme	doome	*doom*	*doom*
Acc.	dōm	doom		doom
Plur. Nom., Acc.	dōmas	doomes		doomes
Gen.	dōma	doome	*doomes*	*doomes*
Dat.	dōmum[56]	doome(n)[57]	*doomes*	*doomes*

52. ende, masculine:

Sing. Nom.	ende	ende		ende
Gen.	endes	endes		endes
Dat.	ende	ende		ende
Acc.	ende	ende		ende
Plur. Nom., Acc.	endas	endes		endes
Gen.	enda	ende	*endes*	*endes*
Dat.	endum	ende(n)	*endes*	*endes*

53. sunu, masculine:

Sing. Nom.	sunu	sune		sone[58]
Gen.	suna	sune	*sunes*	*sones*
Dat.	suna	sune		sone
Acc.	sunu	sune		sone
Plur. Nom., Acc.	suna	sune	*sunes*	*sones*
Gen.	suna	sune	*sunes*	*sones*
Dat.	sunum	sune(n)	*sunes*	*sones*

[56] See 46, 1 above for change of OE final m to ME final n in unstressed syllables.

[57] As stated above in section 46, 1 the ending -en was very frequently reduced to -e thru the loss of the final n; in these tables, therefore, the ending is printed -e(n).

[58] In this column the forms are given in their late Middle English spelling; in the two former columns the forms are given in their early Middle English spelling.

NOUNS

	OLD ENGLISH	MIDDLE ENGLISH		
		Historical forms	Analogical forms	Late ME
54. lufu, feminine:				
Sing. Nom.	lufu	luve		love
Gen.	lufe	luve	*luves*	*loves*
Dat.	lufe	luve		love
Acc.	lufe	luve		love
Plur. Nom., Acc.	lufa	luve	*luves*	*loves*
Gen.	lufa	luve	*luves*	*loves*
Dat.	lufum	luve(n)	*luves*	*loves*
55. hwil, feminine:				
Sing. Nom.	hwil	hwil	*hwile*	*while*
Gen.	hwile	hwile	*hwiles*	*whiles*
Dat.	hwile	hwile		while
Acc.	hwile	hwile		while
Plur. Nom., Acc.	hwila	hwile	*hwiles*	*whiles*
Gen.	hwila	hwile	*hwiles*	*whiles*
Dat.	hwilum	hwile(n)	*hwiles*	*whiles*
56. lim, neuter:				
Sing. Nom.	lim	lim		lim
Gen.	limes	limes		limes
Dat.	lime	lime	*lim*	*lim*
Acc.	lim	lim		lim
Plur. Nom., Acc.	limu	lime	*limes*	*limes*
Gen.	lima	lime	*limes*	*limes*
Dat.	limum	lime(n)	*limes*	*limes*
57. hors, neuter:				
Sing. Nom.	hors	hors		hors
Gen.	horses	horses		horses
Dat.	horse	horse	*hors*	*hors*
Acc.	hors	hors		hors
Plur. Nom., Acc.	hors	hors	*horses*	*horses*
Gen.	horsa	horse	*horses*	*horses*
Dat.	horsum	horse(n)	*horses*	*horses*

NOUNS

	OLD ENGLISH	MIDDLE ENGLISH		
		Historical forms	Analogical forms	Late ME
58. wite, neuter:				
Sing. Nom.	**wite**	wite		wite
Gen.	**wites**	wites		wites
Dat.	**wite**	wite		wite
Acc.	**wite**	wite		wite
Plur. Nom., Acc.	**witu**	wite	*wites*	*wites*
Gen.	**wita**	wite	*wites*	*wites*
Dat.	**witum**	wite(n)	*wites*	*wites*
59. hunta, weak masculine:				
Sing. Nom.	**hunta**	hunte		hunte
Gen.	**huntan**	hunte(n)	*huntes*	*huntes*
Dat.	**huntan**	hunte(n)	*hunte*[59]	*hunte*
Acc.	**huntan**	hunte(n)	*hunte*[59]	*hunte*
Plur. Nom., Acc.	**huntan**	hunte(n)	*huntes*	*huntes*
Gen.	**huntena**	huntene	*huntes*	*huntes*
Dat.	**huntum**	hunte(n)	*huntes*	*huntes*
60. sunne, weak feminine:				
Sing. Nom.	**sunne**	sunne		sonne
Gen.	**sunnan**	sunne(n)	*sunnes*	*sonnes*
Dat.	**sunnan**	sunne(n)	*sunne*[59]	*sonne*
Acc.	**sunnan**	sunne(n)	*sunne*[59]	*sonne*
Plur. Nom., Acc.	**sunnan**	sunne(n)	*sunnes*	*sonnes*
Gen.	**sunnena**	sunnene	*sunnes*	*sonnes*
Dat.	**sunnum**	sunne(n)	*sunnes*	*sonnes*

[59] Inasmuch as the early Middle English ending -en was always liable to undergo reduction to -e thru loss of final n (see note 57 above), sound change was no doubt an important factor in the establishment of this form.

	OLD ENGLISH	MIDDLE ENGLISH		
		Historical forms	Analogical forms	Late ME

61. ĕare, weak neuter:

		OE	Historical	Analogical	Late ME
Sing.	Nom.	ĕare	ere		ere
	Gen.	ēaran	ere(n)	eres	eres
	Dat.	ēaran	ere(n)	ere[59]	ere
	Acc.	ĕare	ere		ere
Plur.	Nom., Acc.	ēaran	ere(n)	eres	eres
	Gen.	ēarena	erene	eres	eres
	Dat.	ēarum	ere(n)	eres	eres

62. An analysis of the tables given above shows that the analogical changes that took place in the inflection of nouns were these:

1. The nominative singular became identical with the accusative singular in the strong feminine nouns ending in a consonant, which in Old English had different forms for the two cases.

2. The ending -es became the ending of the genitive singular of nouns which in Old English had other endings.

3. The dative singular became identical with the accusative singular in those nouns which had different forms for the two cases.

4. The accusative singular became identical with the nominative singular in the weak masculine and feminine nouns, which in Old English had different forms for the two cases.

5. The ending -es became the ending of the nominative-accusative plural of those nouns which in Old English had other endings.

6. The genitive and dative plural became identical with the nominative-accusative plural.

63. Retention and Extension of the Weak Noun Inflection. One other statement is needed, however, to complete this account of the Middle English noun inflections. A few nouns that belonged to the Old English weak declension retained their weak inflection, at least in part, even in Late Middle English. The development of this type of inflec-

---

[59] Inasmuch as the early Middle English ending -en was always liable to undergo reduction to -e thru loss of final n (see note 57 above), sound change was no doubt an important factor in the establishment of this form.

tion, as exemplified by Old English **oxa** (*ox*), is shown in the following table:

	OLD ENGLISH	MIDDLE ENGLISH		
		Historical forms	Analogical forms	Late ME
Sing. Nom.	**oxa**	**oxe**		**oxe**
Gen.	**oxan**	**oxe(n)**	*oxes*	*oxes*
Dat.	**oxan**	**oxe(n)**	*oxe*[59]	*oxe*
Acc.	**oxan**	**oxe(n)**	*oxe*[59]	*oxe*
Plur. Nom., Acc.	**oxan**	**oxe(n)**		**oxen**
Gen.	**oxena**	**oxene**	*oxen*	*oxen*
Dat.	**oxum**	**oxe(n)**		**oxen**

Sometimes this type of inflection was extended to nouns that were not weak nouns in Old English; as the plural of **sune** we sometimes find, for example, **sunen** instead of **sune** or **sunes**. Likewise the weak genitive plural ending -ene was sometimes extended to nouns that were not weak in Old English; e.g., **kingene king** *king of kings*.

64. Summary. The endings, both historical and analogical, which appear (in various combinations) in the **strong** noun declensions are as follows:

	Historical	Analogical
Sing. Nom.	—, -e	-e
Gen.	-es, -e	-es
Dat.	-e	—
Acc.	—, -e	
Plur. Nom., Acc.	-es, -e, —	-es
Gen.	-e	-es
Dat.	-e(n)	-es

ADJECTIVES

65. Declension of Adjectives. In Old English, as in Modern German, every adjective was inflected according to either one of two declensions, the strong or the weak. The weak declension was used if the adjective was preceded by a definite article, a demonstrative, or a posses-

---

[59] Inasmuch as the early Middle English ending -en was always liable to undergo reduction to -e thru loss of final n (see note 57 above), sound change was no doubt an important factor in the establishment of this form.

ADJECTIVES

sive, or if the adjective modified a noun used in direct address; the strong declension was used except under conditions that required the use of the weak. In Middle English the two declensions of the adjective were retained, but with much simplification of forms. As in the declension of nouns, the simplification that took place in the inflection of adjectives was the result of two causes, sound change and analogy. The historical development is shown in the tables printed below:

66. Strong Declension.

	OLD ENGLISH	MIDDLE ENGLISH		
		Historical forms (Early ME)	Analogical forms	Late ME
Masculine:				
Sing. Nom.	gōd	good		good
Gen.	gōdes	goodes	good	good
Dat.	gōdum	goode(n)	good	good
Acc.	gōdne	goodne	good	good
Plur. Nom., Acc.	gōde	goode		goode
Gen.	gōdra	goodre, gooder	goode	goode
Dat.	gōdum	goode(n)	goode[60]	goode
Femine:				
Sing. Nom.	gōd	good		good
Gen.	gōdre	goodre, gooder	good	good
Dat.	gōdre	goodre, gooder	good	good
Acc.	gōde	goode	good	good
Plur. Nom., Acc.	gōda	goode		goode
Gen.	gōdra	goodre, gooder	goode	goode
Dat.	gōdum	goode(n)	goode[60]	goode
Neuter:				
Sing. Nom.	gōd	good		good
Gen.	gōdes	goodes	good	good
Dat.	gōdum	goode(n)	good	good
Acc.	gōd	good		good
Plur. Nom., Acc.	gōde	goode		goode
Gen.	gōdra	goodre, gooder	goode	goode
Dat.	gōdum	goode(n)	goode[60]	goode

[60] Inasmuch as the early Middle English ending -en was always liable to undergo reduction to -e thru loss of final n (see note 57 above), sound change was no doubt an important factor in the establishment of this form.

67. Weak Declension.

	OLD ENGLISH	MIDDLE ENGLISH		
		Historical forms (Early ME)	Anological forms	Late ME
Masculine:				
Sing. Nom.	gōda	goode		goode
Gen.	gōdan	goode(n)	goode[50]	goode
Dat.	gōdan	goode(n)	goode[50]	goode
Acc.	gōdan	goode(n)	goode[50]	goode
Plur. Nom., Acc.	gōdan	goode(n)	goode[50]	goode
Gen.	gōdena	goodene	goode	goode
Dat.	gōdum	goode(n)	goode[50]	goode
Feminine:				
Sing. Nom.	gōde	goode		goode
Gen.	gōdan	goode(n)	goode[50]	goode
Dat.	gōdan	goode(n)	goode[50]	goode
Acc.	gōdan	goode(n)	goode[50]	goode
Plur. Nom., Acc.	gōdan	goode(n)	goode[50]	goode
Gen.	gōdena	goodene	goode	goode
Dat.	gōdum	goode(n)	goode[50]	goode
Neuter:				
Sing. Nom.	gōde	goode		goode
Gen.	gōdan	goode(n)	goode[50]	goode
Dat.	gōdan	goode(n)	goode[50]	goode
Acc.	gōde	goode		goode
Plur. Nom., Acc.	gōdan	goode(n)	goode[50]	goode
Gen.	gōdena	goodene	goode	goode
Dat.	gōdum	goode(n)	goode[50]	goode

PRONOUNS

68. Declension of Pronouns. The development of the Middle English pronouns is more complex than that of the noun and adjective inflections. One reason is that the Old English pronouns had a good many variant forms, any one of which might become the basis of a corresponding Middle English form. Another reason is that pronouns are

---

[50] Inasmuch as the early Middle English ending -en was always liable to reduction to -e thru loss of final n (see note 57 above), sound change was no doubt an important factor in the establishment of this form.

often weakly stressed, and the sound changes that take place in weakly stressed syllables are not always the same as those that take place in strongly stressed syllables. In the following tables, as in those given above, the historical forms that developed by sound change are printed in Roman type, analogical forms in italics.[61]

69. First Personal Pronoun.

	OLD ENGLISH	MIDDLE ENGLISH
Sing. Nom.	ič	ich [itʃ], I [i]
Gen.	mīn	mi(n)
Dat.	mē	me
Acc.	mē	me
Plur. Nom.	wē	we
Gen.	ūre	ure
Dat., Acc.	ūs	us [ūs], [us]

70. Second Personal Pronoun.

Sing. Nom.	þū	þu
Gen.	þīn	þi(n)
Dat.	þē	þe
Acc.	þē	þe
Plur. Nom.	ġē	ȝe [jē]
Gen.	ēower	eower [ēouǝr], ower [ǭuǝr], ȝur [jūr]
Dat., Acc.	ēow	eow [ēou], ow [ǭu], ȝu [jū]

71. Third Personal Pronoun.

	OLD ENGLISH	MIDDLE ENGLISH	Analogical forms
Masculine Singular:			
Nom.	hē	he	
Gen.	his	his	
Dat.	him	him	
Acc.	hine	hine	*him*
Feminine Singular:			
Nom.	hēo, hī	heo, he [hē], ho [hǭ], hi [hī]	
Gen.	hire	hire	*here*
Dat.	hire	hire	*here*
Acc.	hī, hēo	hi [hī]; heo, he [hē], ho [hǭ]	*hire, here*

[61] These tables do not attempt to give *all* the Middle English pronominal forms, but only the commoner and more characteristic ones. No account is taken of mere variations of spelling.

Neuter Singular:

Nom.	hit	hit	
Gen.	his	his	
Dat.	him	him	*hit*
Acc.	hit	hit	

Plural (all genders):

Nom.	hī, hēo	hi [hī]; heo, he [hē], ho [hō]	
Gen.	hira, heora	hire, here	
Dat.	him, heom	him, hem	
Acc.	hī, hēo	hi [hī]; heo, he, [hē], ho [hō]	*him, hem*

72. Demonstrative Pronoun and Definite Article.

	OLD ENGLISH	MIDDLE ENGLISH	Analogical forms
Masculine Singular:			
Nom.	sē	se	þe, þat
Gen.	þæs	þes, þas	þe, þat
Dat.	þǣm, þām	þen, þan	þe, þat
Acc.	þone, þæne	þone, þene, þane	þe, þat
Inst.	þȳ, þon, þē	þi, þon, þe	
Feminine Singular:			
Nom.	sēo	seo, se	þe, þat
Gen.	þǣre	þere, þare	þe, þat
Dat.	þǣre	þere, þare	þe, þat
Acc.	þā	þo [þō], þa [þa]	þe, þat
Neuter Singular:			
Nom.	þæt	þet, þat	þe
Gen.	þæs	þes, þas	þe, þat
Dat.	þǣm, þām	þen, þan	þe, þat
Acc.	þæt	þet, þat	þe
Inst.	þȳ, þon, þē	þi, þon, þe	
Plural (all genders):			
Nom.	þā	þo [þō], þa [þa]	þe
Gen.	þāra, þǣra	þare, þere	þe, þo
Dat.	þǣm, þām	þen, þan	þe, þo
Acc.	þā	þo, þa	þe

VERBS

73. Weak Verbs. In Middle English, as in Old English and all other Germanic languages, there are two conjugations of verbs, the strong and the weak. Weak verbs form their preterit by means of a suffix containing **d** or **t** followed by endings indicative of person and number. From the point of view of their development in Middle English, we may say that there were two types of weak verbs in Old English. Verbs of the first type had preterits ending in **-ede** or **-ode** and past participles ending in **-ed** or **-od**; for example,

fremman (*make*)	fremede	fremed
erian (*plow*)	erede	ered
lufian (*love*)	lufode	lufod

In Middle English the distinction between **lufian**, with preterit in **-ode**, and **fremman** and **erian**, with preterits in **-ede**, was done away with by the process of sound change, so that the earliest Middle English forms of these verbs were

fremme(n)	fremede	fremed
erie(n)	erede	ered
luvie(n)	luvede	luved

These verbs, which we shall call weak verbs of Type I, therefore had in Middle English preterits ending in **-ede** and past participles ending in **-ed**. In early Middle English the infinitive of these verbs ended in **-e(n)** or **-ie(n)**, but in late Middle English, by the process of analogy, the ending **-ie(n)** was displaced by the commoner ending **-e(n)**.

Old English verbs of the second type had preterits ending in **-de** or **-te** and past participles ending in **-ed**, **-d**, or **-t**; for example:

dēman (*judge*)	dēmde	dēmed
fēlan (*feel*)	fēlde	fēled
fēdan (*feed*)	fēdde	fēded, fēdd
wendan (*turn*)	wende	wended, wend
cēpan (*keep*)	cēpte	cēped
mētan (*meet*)	mētte	mēted, mētt
settan (*set*)	sette	seted, sett
sēċan (*seek*)	sōhte	sōht
þenċan (*think*)	þōhte	þōht

In Middle English these verbs developed, according to the regular laws of sound change, as follows:

deme(n) [dēmən]	demde [dēmdə]	demed [dēməd]
fele(n) [fēlən]	felte [fɛltə]	feled [fēləd]
fede(n) [fēdən]	fedde [fɛddə]	fed [fɛd]
wende(n) [wɛndən]	wente [wɛntə]	went [wɛnt]
kepe(n) [kēpən]	kepte [kɛptə]	keped [kēpəd]
mete(n) [mētən]	mette [mɛttə]	met [mɛt]
sette(n) [sɛttən]	sette [sɛttə]	set [sɛt]
seche(n) [sētʃən]	soughte [souhtə]	sought [souht]
þenche(n) [þɛntʃən]	þoughte [þouhtə]	þought [þouht]

These verbs, which we shall call weak verbs of Type II, therefore had in Middle English preterits ending in -de or -te and past participles ending in -ed, d, or t. It will be observed that (in accordance with the sound law stated above in section 43, 1a) the long vowels of **felen, feden, kepen,** and **meten** are shortened in the preterit, where they were followed by a double consonant or a combination of consonants.

74. Strong Verbs. Strong verbs form their preterit, not by the addition of a suffix, but by means of a change in the vowel of the stem of the verb. This change is called "ablaut," and the strong verbs are frequently called "ablaut verbs." The preterit plural of these verbs usually has a different vowel from the preterit singular; the principal parts therefore are the infinitive, the preterit indicative first person singular, the preterit indicative plural, and the past participle.

In Old English there were seven classes of strong verbs; the principal parts of verbs representative of these seven classes are as follows:

I. rīdan (*ride*)	rād	ridon	riden
II. crēopan (*creep*)	crēap	crupon	cropen
III. bindan (*bind*)	band, bond	bundon	bunden
helpan (*help*)	healp	hulpon	holpen
sterfan (*die*)	stearf	sturfon	storfen
IV. beran (*bear*)	bær	bǣron	boren
V. specan (*speak*)	spæc	spǣcon	specen
VI. scacan (*shake*)	scōc	scōcon	scacen
VII. slǣpan (*sleep*)	slēp	slēpon	slǣpen
healdan (*hold*)	hēold	hēoldon	healden

By the operation of the sound changes which have been explained in sections 42 and 43, these Old English forms developed into the following Middle English forms:[62]

I. ride(n) [rīdən]	rod [rǭd]	ride(n) [ridən]	ride(n) [ridən]
II. crepe(n) [krēpən]	creep [krēp]	crupe(n) [krupən]	crope(n) [krǭpən]
III. binde(n) [bindən]	band [band]	bunde(n) [bŭndən]	bunde(n) [bŭndən]
	bond [bǭnd]		
helpe(n) [hęlpən]	halp [halp]	hulpe(n) [hulpən]	holpe(n) [hǫlpən]
sterve(n) [stęrvən]	starf [starf]	sturve(n) [sturvən]	storve(n) [stǫrvən]
IV. bere(n) [bẹ̄rən]	bar [bar]	bere(n) [bērən]	bore(n) [bǭrən]
V. speke(n) [spẹ̄kən]	spak [spak]	speke(n) [spēkən]	speke(n) [spẹ̄kən]
VI. shake(n) [šākən]	shook [šōk]	shooke(n) [šōkən]	shake(n) [šākən]
VII. slepe(n) [slēpən]	sleep [slēp]	sleepe(n) [slēpən]	slepe(n) [slēpən]
holde(n) [hǭldən]	heeld [hēld]	heelde(n) [hēldən]	holde(n) [hǭldən]

75. Analogical Forms. The forms that developed from the Old English forms by sound change are those that occur in early Middle English, but in later Middle English we meet with a good many analogical forms. The most important results of analogy were these:

1. Strong verbs often acquired weak preterits; e.g., **crepte** [kręptə], **slepte** [slęptə], in place of **creep, sleep**.

2. The vowel of the preterit plural was often substituted for the vowel of the preterit singular; e.g., **beer** [bēr], with the vowel of the preterit plural, displaced **bar**.

3. The vowel of the preterit singular was often substituted for the vowel of the preterit plural; e.g., **bare(n)** [bārən], with the vowel of the preterit singular (lengthened when it came to stand in an open syllable),[63] displaced **bere(n)** [bērən].

4. The vowel of the past participle was often substituted for the vowel of the preterit plural; e.g., **crope(n)** [krǭpən], with the vowel of the past participle, displaced **crupe(n)**.

---

[62] The Middle English forms here given are those of the Midland dialect; the Old English forms given above are those of the West-Saxon dialect (see note 37 above) The Mercian dialect of Old English, which was that from which the Midland dialect of Middle English was derived, had some forms which differed from those of the West-Saxon dialect. In place of beron, specon, and slepan it had beron, specon and slepan, and in place of healdan and healden it had haldan and halden.

[63] See section 43, 1b, above.

5. In the past participles of verbs of Class V the vowel **o** [ǭ] was substituted for the original vowel **e**, from the analogy of the past participle of verbs of Class IV; e.g., **spoke(n)** [spǭkən], with the vowel of **bore(n)** [bǭrən], displaced **speke(n)** [spḕkən].

76. Endings of Weak Verbs. The historical development of the Middle English forms of the weak verb is shown in the tables printed below. Weak verbs of Type I are exemplified by Old English **erian** (*plow*) and **lufian** (*love*); weak verbs of Type II are exemplified by Old English **dēman** (*judge*).

	OLD ENGLISH	MIDDLE ENGLISH Historical forms	Analogical forms
Pres. Ind. Sing. 1	erie	erie	*ere*
2	erest	erest	
3	ereþ	ereþ	
Plur.	eriaþ	erieþ	*ereþ, ere(n)*[64]
Pret. Ind. Sing. 1	erede	erede	
2	eredest	eredest	
3	erede	erede	
Plur.	eredon	erede(n)	
Pres. Subj. Sing.	erie	erie	*ere*
Plur.	erien	erie(n)	*ere(n)*
Pret. Subj. Sing.	erede	erede	
Plur.	ereden	erede(n)	
Pres. Imp. Sing. 2	ere	ere	
Plur. 2	eriaþ	erieþ	*ereþ*
Infinitive	erian	erie(n)	*ere(n)*
Gerund	tō erienne	to eriene	*to erene, to ere(n)*
Pres. Participle	eriende	eriende, eriinde[65]	*erende, erinde,*[65] *eringe*
Past Participle	ered	ered	

[64] The ending -e(n) in the present indicative plural is a characteristic of the Midland dialect; the ending -eþ is a characteristic of the Southern dialect.

[65] The ending -inde is a characteristic of the Southern dialect, the ending -ende of the Midland dialect.

VERBS

	OLD ENGLISH	MIDDLE ENGLISH	
		Historical forms	Analogical forms
Pres. Ind. Sing. 1	lufie	luvie, luvi	luve
2	lufast	luvest	
3	lufaþ	luveþ	
Plur.	lufiaþ	luvieþ	luveþ, luve(n)[64]
Pret. Ind. Sing. 1	lufode	luvede	
2	lufodest	luvedest	
3	lufode	luvede	
Plur.	lufodon	luvede(n)	
Pres. Subj. Sing.	lufie	luvie, luvi	luve
Plur.	lufien	luvie(n), luvi(n)	luve(n)
Pret. Subj. Sing.	lufode	luvede	
Plur.	lufoden	luvede(n)	
Pres. Imp. Sing. 2	lufa	luve	
Plur. 2	lufiaþ	luvieþ	luveþ
Infinitive	lufian	luvie(n), luvi(n)	luve(n)
Gerund	tō lufienne	to luviene	to luvene, to luve(n)
Pres. Participle	lufiende	luviende, luviünde[65]	luvende, luvinde,[65] luvinge
Past Participle	lufod	luved	
Pres. Ind. Sing. 1	dēme	deme	
2	dēmest, dēmst	demest, demst	
3	dēmeþ, dēmþ	demeþ, demþ	
Plur.	dēmaþ	demeþ	deme(n)[64]
Pret. Ind. Sing. 1	dēmde	demde	
2	dēmdest	demdest	
3	dēmde	demde	
Plur.	dēmdon	demde(n)	
Pres. Subj. Sing.	dēme	deme	
Plur.	dēmen	deme(n)	

[64] The ending -e(n) in the present indicative plural is a characteristic of the Midland dialect; the ending -eþ is a characteristic of the Southern dialect.

[65] The ending -inde is a characteristic of the Southern dialect, the ending -ende of the Midland dialect.

	OLD ENGLISH	MIDDLE ENGLISH Historical forms	Analogical forms
Pret. Subj. Sing.	dēmde	demde	
Plur.	dēmden	demde(n)	
Pres. Imp. Sing. 2	dēm	dem	*deme*
Plur. 2	dēmaþ	demeþ	
Infinitive	dēman	deme(n)	
Gerund	tō dēmenne	to demene	*to deme(n)*
Pres. Participle	dēmende	demende, deminde[65]	*deminge*
Past Participle	dēmed	demed	

77. Endings of Strong Verbs. The historical development of the Middle English forms of the strong verb, exemplified by Old English **rīdan** (*ride*) and **bindan** (*bind*), is shown in the tables printed below.

	OLD ENGLISH	MIDDLE ENGLISH Historical forms	Analogical forms
Pres. Ind. Sing. 1	rīde	ride	
2	rīdest, rītst	ridest, ritst	
3	rīdeþ, rītt	rideþ, rit	
Plur.	rīdaþ	rideþ	*ride(n)*[66]
Pret. Ind. Sing. 1	rād	rood	
2	ride[67]	ride	*rood*
3	rād	rood	
Plur.	ridon	ride(n)	
Pres. Subj. Sing.	rīde	ride	
Plur.	rīden	ride(n)	
Pret. Subj. Sing.	ride	ride	
Plur.	riden	ride(n)	
Pres. Imp. Sing. 2	rīd	rid	
Plur. 2	rīdaþ	rideþ	

[65] The ending -inde is a characteristic of the Southern dialect, the ending -ende of the Midland dialect.

[66] The ending -e(n) in the present indicative plural is a characteristic of the Midland dialect; the ending -eþ is a characteristic of the Southern dialect.

[67] It should be observed that the preterit indicative 2 singular of the strong verbs has the vowel of the preterit plural.

VERBS

	OLD ENGLISH	MIDDLE ENGLISH	
		Historical forms	Analogical forms
Infinitive	rīdan	ride(n)	
Gerund	tō rīdenne	to ridene	*to ride(n)*
Pres. Participle	rīdende	ridende, ridinde[65]	*ridinge*
Past Participle	riden	ride(n)	
Pres. Ind. Sing. 1	binde	binde	
2	bindest, bintst	bindest, bintst	
3	bindeþ, bint	bindeþ, bint	
Plur.	bindaþ	bindeþ	*binde(n)*[66]
Pret. Ind. Sing. 1	band, bond	band, bond	
2	bunde[67]	bunde	*band, bond*
3	band, bond	band, bond	
Plur.	bundon	bunde(n)	
Pres. Subj. Sing.	binde	binde	
Plur.	binden	binde(n)	
Pret. Subj. Sing.	bunde	bunde	
Plur.	bunden	bunde(n)	
Pres. Imp. Sing. 2	bind	bind	
Plur. 2	bindaþ	bindeþ	
Infinitive	bindan	binde(n)	
Gerund	tō bindenne	to bindene	*to binde(n)*
Pres. Participle	bindende	bindende, bindinde[65]	*bindinge*
Past Participle	bunden	bunde(n)	

78. Preteritive-Present Verbs. The preteritive-present (or strong-weak) verbs have **present** indicatives which are like the **preterit** indicatives of strong verbs in that they have no ending in the first and third persons singular and have the ending -e(n) (from Old English -on) in

---

[65] The ending -inde is a characteristic of the Southern dialect, the ending -ende of the Midland dialect.

[66] The ending -e(n) in the present indicative plural is a characteristic of the Midland dialect, the -eþ ending is that of the Southern dialect.

[67] It should be observed that the preterit indicative 2 singular of the strong verbs has the vowel of the preterit plural.

the plural. The **preterits** of these verbs are **weak**. The indicative forms of Middle English **shal**, for example, are as follows:

    Pres. Ind. Sing. 1 **shal**
          2 **shalt**
          3 **shal**
      Plur. **shule(n)**
    Pret. Ind. Sing. 1 **sholde**
          2 **sholdest**
          3 **sholde**
      Plur. **sholde(n)**

The most important of the preteritive-present verbs are:

  owen, *own, be under obligation*
  cunnen, *know, be able*
  muwen, *be able*
  moten, *be permitted, be under obligation*
  shulen, *be under obligation, be about to*
  witen, *know*

79. The historical development of the preteritive-present verbs is shown in the following tables:

OLD ENGLISH   MIDDLE ENGLISH

          Historical Analogical
          forms   forms

Pres. Ind. Sing. 1 **āh, āg** **ouh** [ǫuh], **ow** [ǫu] *owe* [ǫuə]
     2 **āhst** **ouhst** [ǫuhst] *owest* [ǫuəst]
     3 **āh, āg** **ouh** [ǫuh], **ow** [ǫu] *oweþ* [ǫuəþ]
   Plur. **āgon** **owe(n)** [ǫuən] *oweþ* [ǫuəþ][66]
Pret. Ind. Sing. 1 **āhte** **ouhte** [ǫuhtə]
Infinitive   **āgan** **owe(n)** [ǫuən]

Pres. Ind. Sing. 1 **cann, conn** can, con
     2 **canst, const** canst, const
     3 **cann, conn** can, con
   Plur. **cunnon** cunne(n)

[66] This form occurs only in the Southern dialect.

VERBS

	OLD ENGLISH	MIDDLE ENGLISH	
		Historical forms	Analogical forms
Pret. Ind. Sing. 1	cūþe	cuþe [kūðə]	*cude* [kūdə]
Infinitive	cunnan	cunne(n)	
Pres. Ind. Sing. 1	mæġ	mai, mei	
2	meaht, miht	maht, maiht, meiht, mauht, mouht, miht	*maist*
3	mæġ	mai, mei	
Plur.	magon, mugon[69]	mawe(n), muwe(n)	
Pret. Ind. Sing. 1	meahte, mihte	mahte, maihte, meihte, mauhte, mouhte, mihte	*muhte*
Infinitive	magan, mugan[70]	mawe(n), muwe(n)	
Pres. Ind. Sing. 1	mōt	mot	
2	mōst	most	
3	mōt	mot	
Plur.	mōton	mote(n)	
Pret. Ind. Sing. 1	mōste	moste	
Infinitive	mōtan	mote(n)	
Pres. Ind. Sing. 1	sceal	shal, shel	
2	scealt	shalt, shelt	
3	sceal	shal, shel	
Plur.	sculon	shule(n)	
Pret. Ind. Sing. 1	scolde	sholde	*shulde*
Infinitive	sculan	shule(n)	
Pres. Ind. Sing. 1	wāt	wot	
2	wāst	wost	
3	wāt	wot	
Plur.	witon	wite(n)	
Pret. Ind. Sing. 1	wiste	wiste, wuste	
Infinitive	witan	wite(n)	

[69] The form **mugon** is not recorded in Old English, but is inferred from the Middle English forms.

[70] The form **mugan** is not recorded in Old English, but is inferred from the Middle English forms.

VERBS

80. Anomalous Verbs. The historical development of the Middle English verb **bee(n)**, *be*, was as follows:

	OLD ENGLISH		MIDDLE ENGLISH		
			Historical forms		Analogical forms
Pres. Ind. Sing. 1	eom, eam[71]	bēo	em, am	be	
2	eart	bist	art	bist	*beest*
3	is	biþ	is	biþ	*beeþ*
Plur.	sindon, earon[72]	bēoþ	sinde(n), are(n)[73]	beeþ	*bee(n)*[74]
Pret. Ind. Sing. 1	wæs		wes, was		
2	wǣre		were		
3	wæs		wes, was		
Plur.	wǣron		were(n)		
Pres. Subj. Sing.	sīe	bēo	si	be	
Plur.	sīen	bēon	si(n)	bee(n)	
Pret. Subj. Sing.	wǣre		were		
Plur.	wǣren		were(n)		
Pres. Imp. Sing. 2		bēo		be	
Plur. 2		bēoþ		beeþ	
Infinitive		bēon		bee(n)	

The historical development of the Middle English verbs **don**, *do*, and **willen**, *will*, in the indicative was as follows:

	OLD ENGLISH	MIDDLE ENGLISH	
		Historical forms	Analogical forms
Pres. Ind. Sing. 1	dō	do	
2	dēst	dest	*dost*
3	dēþ	deþ	*doþ*
Plur.	dōþ	doþ	*do(n)*[75]

[71] **eam** is the Mercian form, **eom** the West-Saxon.
[72] **earon** is the Mercian form, **sindon** was used in all the Old English dialects.
[73] **are(n)** was not used in the Southern dialect, but only in the Midland and North.
[74] **bee(n)** is a Midland form; it was not used in the South.
[75] **do(n)** is the Midland form; it was not used in the South.

VERBS

	OLD ENGLISH	MIDDLE ENGLISH	
		Historical forms	Analogical forms
Pret. Ind. Sing. 1	dyde	dide, dude [dydə]	
2	dydest	didest, dudest	
3	dyde	dide, dude	
Plur.	dydon	dide(n), dude(n)	
Past Participle	dōn	don	
Pres. Ind. Sing. 1	wille	wille, wulle	*wile, wule*
2	wilt	wilt, wult	
3	wile	wile, wule	*wille, wulle*
Plur.	willaþ	willeþ, wulleþ	*wille(n), wulle(n)*[76]
Pret. Ind. Sing. 1	wolde	wolde	*wulde*
2	woldest	woldest	*wuldest*
3	wolde	wolde	*wulde*
Plur.	woldon	wolde(n)	*wulde(n)*

[76] **wille(n)** and **wulle(n)** are Midland forms.

PART V

MIDDLE ENGLISH DIALECTS

81. Distribution of the Middle English Dialects. There were four chief dialects of Middle English, the Southern, the Kentish, the Midland, and the Northern. The Southern dialect was spoken south of the Thames, except in Kent. The Midland dialect was spoken in the district which lay (roughly) between the Thames on the south and the mouth of the Humber on the north. The Northern dialect was spoken in the district which lay (roughly) north of the mouth of the Humber; this district included Yorkshire and its adjacent counties and the lowlands of Scotland. The territory of the Midland dialect is further divided into the North and the South Midland and the East and the West Midland.

82. The Southern Dialect. The most important characteristics of the Southern dialect are the following:

I. Vowel Sounds. The development of the Old English vowels and diphthongs in the Midland dialect of Middle English has been given above in 42. The development of the Old English vowel sounds in the Southern dialect was the same as in the Midland dialect except that Old English ȳ and y, which had the sound of [ȳ] and [y], preserved their original quality in the Southern dialect, tho the sounds were spelled in Middle English with u or ui instead of y; e.g., OE fȳr, Southern ME vur, vuir; OE fyllan, Southern ME vullen.[77]

---

[77] In many words the Southern dialect has [ę̄] where the Midland and Northern dialects have [ē]. This dialect difference originated in Old English, for West-Saxon ǣ appears in the Anglian dialect as ē unless the ǣ is the result of umlaut. In Southern Middle English we therefore have [dę̄d] from West-Saxon dǣd, but in the Midland and Northern dialects we have [dēd] from Anglian dēd. In all three dialects, however, we have Middle English [hę̄þ] from West-Saxon and Anglian hǣþ. See note 37 above. The Anglian dialect of Old English included the Mercian dialect, from which the Midland dialect of Middle English was derived, and the Northumbrian dialect, from which the Northern dialect of Middle English was derived.

II. **Consonant Sounds.** The Old English initial voiceless spirants [f], [s], and [þ] changed to the corresponding voiced spirants [v], [z], and [ð]; e.g., OE for, Southern ME vor; OE song, Southern ME zong; OE þæt [þæt], Southern ME þat [ðat].[78]

III. **Final e.** Final e was retained in pronunciation thruout the fourteenth century.

IV. **Inflections.**

  1. Nouns.

    (a) The historical forms of the noun declensions (see 49 ff. above) were displaced only slowly by analogical forms. Genitive and dative singulars in e, nominative, genitive, and accusative plurals in e, and dative plurals in e(n) are common in texts of the thirteenth century and occur occasionally in texts of the fourteenth century.

    (b) The distinctions of grammatical gender were maintained with a considerable degree of correctness thruout the first half of the thirteenth century, and relics of grammatical gender are found even in texts of the first half of the fourteenth century.

  2. Adjectives.

    The historical forms of the genitive, dative, and accusative in the strong adjective declension (see 65 ff. above) were displaced only slowly by analogical forms; the historical forms occur frequently in texts of the first half of the thirteenth century.

  3. Pronouns.

    (a) The historical forms of the genitive, dative, and accusative of the definite article and demonstrative þe (se), þat[79] (see 72 above) were displaced only slowly by analogical

---

[78] The initial [v] is indicated pretty consistently in the spelling of Southern Middle English texts; the initial [z] is indicated by the spelling of one text only, for the letter z was little used by the Middle English scribes. The initial [ð] is not indicated by spelling at all, for the scribes had no way of distinguishing the sounds of [ð] and [þ] in writing.

[79] In the Southern dialect þat is used as the definite article as well as the demonstrative; in the Midland and Northern dialects þat is used only as the demonstrative.

forms; the historical forms are common in the first half of the thirteenth century and occasional until the middle of the fourteenth century.

(b) The pronouns **ha** (*he, she, they, them*), **hare** (*her, their*), and **ham** (*them*) were in frequent use.

4. Verbs.

(a) The ending of the present indicative plural of strong verbs was -eþ; the ending of the present indicative plural of weak verbs was -eþ or -ieþ.[80]

(b) The ending of the present participle of strong verbs was -inde, later -inge; the ending of the present participle of weak verbs was -inde, later -inge, or -iinde, later -inge.

(c) Weak verbs like **erien** and **luvien** (see 76 above) preserved their historical endings, -ie, -ie(n), etc., thruout the fourteenth century with little substitution of analogical forms.

83. The Kentish Dialect. The characteristics of the Kentish dialect are the same as those of the Southern dialect except with regard to vowel sounds. The development of the Old English vowels and diphthongs in the Kentish dialect differs in the following respects from the development which these sounds underwent in the Southern and Midland dialects:

1. Old English[81] ȳ and y became Kentish [ē] and [ę]; e.g., OE **fȳr**, Kentish ME **ver** [vēr]; OE **fyllan**, Kentish ME **vellen** [vęllən].

2. Old English ēa became in Kentish a sound which is spelled **ea, ia, ya, yea**; the pronunciation of this sound is uncertain, but it is generally supposed to have been a diphthong, not a simple vowel; e.g., OE **strēam**, Kentish ME **stream, striam**, etc.

3. Old English ēo became in Kentish a sound which is spelled **ie, ye i, y**; the pronunciation of this sound is uncertain, but it is generally supposed to have been a diphthong; e.g., OE **bēon**, Kentish ME **bien, byen**, etc.

---

[80] Likewise, **beeþ** is the Southern form of the present indicative plural of **bee(n), be.**

[81] By Old English is meant here the West-Saxon dialect of Old English (see note 37 above). The Kentish dialect of Old English already had ē and e where the West-Saxon and Anglian dialects had ȳ and y.

4. Old English ie[82] (which in the other Middle English dialects generally became [ē]) became in Kentish a sound which is spelled ie, ye; the pronunciation of this sound is uncertain, but it is generally supposed to have been a diphthong; e.g., OE nied, Kentish ME nied, nyed; OE diere, Kentish ME diere, dyere.[83]

84. The Midland Dialect. The most important characteristics of the Midland dialect are the following:

I. Final e. Final e was to a great extent retained in pronunciation thruout the fourteenth century, but apocope of final e began before the end of the thirteenth century.

II. Inflections.

   1. Nouns and Adjectives.

     (a) The analogical changes that took place in the inflection of nouns (see 49 ff. above) and adjectives (see 65 ff.) were carried out before the end of the twelfth century.

     (b) The distinctions of grammatical gender were lost before the end of the twelfth century.

   2. Pronouns.

     (a) The historical forms of the genitive, dative, and accusative of the definite article and demonstrative þe (se), þat (see 72 above) were displaced by analogical forms before the end of the twelfth century.

     (b) The historical forms of the accusative of the third personal pronoun (see 71 above) were displaced by dative forms before the end of the twelfth century.

   3. Verbs.

     (a) The ending of the present indicative plural of strong and weak verbs was -e(n).

---

[82] The diphthong ie occurs only in the West-Saxon dialect of Old English; in place of ie the other dialects had ē, io, or ēo.

[83] The Kentish dialect of Old English had ē where the West-Saxon dialect had ǣ; in many words, therefore, Kentish Middle English has ē where Southern Middle English has ę̄.

(b) The ending of the present participle of strong and weak verbs was -ende, later -inge or -ing.

(c) The historical endings (ie, ie(n), etc.) of weak verbs like **erien** and **luvien** (see 76 above) were for the most part displaced by analogical forms before the end of the twelfth century.

85. Non-Northern Dialect Characteristics. The Southern and the Midland dialects have in common certain characteristics which are not shared by the Northern dialect:

I. Sounds. Old English $\bar{a}$ became [$\bar{o}$] in Southern and Midland Middle English; e.g., OE **stān**, Southern and Midland ME **stoon**.[84]

II. Inflections.

  1. Pronouns.

    (a) Both the Southern and the Midland dialects employed the pronouns **he, hi, ho** (*she, they*); **hem** (*them*); and **hire, here** (*their*).[85]

    (b) Both the early Southern and the early Midland dialects employed the pronoun **his, is** (*her, it, them*).

  2. Verbs.

    (a) The past participle of strong and weak verbs often had the prefix **i, y**, from Old English **ġe**; e.g., **icume(n)**, past participle of **cume(n)**; the prefix is commoner in the Southern dialect, however, than in the Midland.

    (b) The difference of ablaut in the preterit singular and preterit plural which existed in most of the strong verbs was on the whole retained without much disturbance from analogy (see 74 above).

---

[84] Old English æ is often spelled in early Southern and Midland ME with the letter e; e.g., OE **æfter**, early ME **efter**; in later Middle English the sound is almost uniformly spelled with **a**.

[85] The Southern dialect employed these pronouns exclusively, but the Midland dialect also employed **she, sho**; **þei**; **þeir**; **þeim, þem**. See 86, II, 1 below.

86. Non-Southern Dialect Characteristics. The Midland and the Northern dialects have in common certain characteristics which are not shared by the Southern dialect:

I. Sounds. Old English ȳ and ī became [i] and [ī] in Midland and Northern Middle English; e.g., OE fȳr, Midland and Northern ME **fir**; OE **fyllan**, Midland and Northern ME **fillen**.[86]

II. Inflections.

  1. Pronouns.

    (a) Both the Midland and the Northern dialects employed the pronoun **she, sho** (*she*).[87]

    (b) Both the Midland and the Northern dialects employed the pronouns **þei** (*they*); **þeir** (*their*); **þeim, þem** (*them*).[88]

  2. Verbs.

    (a) Both the Midland and the Northern dialects employed **are(n)** as the present indicative plural of the verb **bee(n)**.[89]

    (b) Both the Midland and the Northern dialects employ **-es** as the ending of the present indicative second and third persons singular of verbs.[90]

---

[86] For the relation between the vowels [ē] and [ɛ̄] in Southern on the one hand and Midland and Northern on the other see note 77 above.

[87] The Northern dialect employed **she, sho**, exclusively as the feminine nominative pronoun, but the Midland dialect employed both **she** and **he, hi, ho** (see 85, II, 1 above). The pronoun **she** was on the whole commonest in the northern part of the Midland territory, the pronoun **he, hi, ho** was commonest in the southern part of the Midland territory.

[88] The Northern dialect employed **þei; þeir; þeim, þem** exclusively as the plural pronouns of the third person, but the Midland dialect also employed **he, hi, ho; hire, here; hem** (see 85, II, 1 above). The pronoun **þei**, etc. was most commonly used in the northern part of the Midland territory, the pronoun **he**, etc. was commonest in the southern part of the Midland territory.

[89] The Midland dialect also employed the form **bee(n)** or **be** as the present indicative plural of **bee(n)**; **are(n)** was commonest in the northern part of the Midland territory.

[90] The ending **-es** was the regular ending of the present indicative second and third persons singular in the Northern dialect (see 87 below); the Midland dialect used regularly the endings **-est** and **-eþ**, and the ending **-es** (especially for the third person) occurs chiefly in the northern part of the Midland territory.

87. The Northern Dialect. The most important characteristics of the Northern dialect are the following:

I. Sounds.

1. Old English **ā** did not change to [ǭ] but remained [ā]; e.g., OE **stān**, Northern ME **stan**, Midland and Southern ME **stoon**. By the end of the fourteenth century, however, the [ā] seems to have become [ę̄] or [ē].[91]

2. [g] and [k] appear in many words which have [j] and [tʃ] in the Southern and Midland dialects; e.g., Northern **gif**, Southern and Midland **yif**; Northern **kirk(e)**, Southern and Midland **chirche**.[92]

3. Old English **sc** [ʃ] became [s] in unaccented syllables and in words that were generally pronounced with little stress; e.g OE **englisc**, Northern ME **inglis**, Southern and Midland ME **english**; OE **sceal**, Northern ME **sal**, Southern and Midland ME **shal**; OE **scolde**, Northern ME **solde, sulde**, Southern and Midland ME **sholde, shulde**.

4. Old English **hw** was spelled in the North **qu**; e.g., OE **hwæt**, Northern ME **quat**, Southern and Midland ME **what, wat**. The sound represented by the **qu** was probably that of a spirant [h] followed by or combined with [w].

II. Final **e** and **e(n)**. Final **e** was entirely lost by about the middle of the fourteenth century. Final **n** of the ending **e(n)** was lost before the beginning of the fourteenth century, except in the past participles of strong verbs.

III. Inflections.[93]

1. Adjectives. With the loss of final **e** about the middle of the fourteenth century, all inflection of the adjective was lost.

---

[91] In the North the long vowels [ā], [ē], and [ō] were often spelled **ai, ay; ei, ey;** and **oi, oy**, particularly in the fifteenth century.

[92] This might better perhaps be considered a non-Southern than a Northern characteristic, for **g** and **k** forms occur also in the Midland territory; they are more numerous, however, in the North.

[93] With regard to the displacement of historical forms by analogical forms in the inflection of nouns, adjectives, pronouns, and verbs, and with regard to the loss of grammatical gender, the Northern dialect was even less conservative than the Midland dialect.

2. Pronouns. The plural of þis (*this*) is þir or þer.

3. Verbs.

(a) The ending of the present indicative first person singular and of the present indicative plural was -es unless the subject of the verb was a personal pronoun which immediately preceded or followed the verb, in which case the verb was without ending or had the ending -e. The present indicative forms of the verb find(e), for example, were

(1) Sing. 1 I find(e)
        2 thou findes   Plur. we, ye, they find(e)
        3 he findes

(2) Sing. 1 I that findes
        2 thou that findes   Plur. we, ye, they that findes
        3 he that findes

(b) The ending of the present participle was -and(e).

(c) The ending of the imperative plural was -es.

(d) The preterit singular and preterit plural of strong verbs had the same vowel, the difference of ablaut which had existed in most of the strong verbs (see 74 above) being done away with by analogy; in most verbs the preterit plural took the vowel of the preterit singular. Thus, with the loss of the ending -e(n), the preterit singular and the preterit plural became identical in form; e.g., Northern **he sang, we sang**, Southern and Midland **he sang, we sunge(n)**.

(e) The ending of the past participle of strong verbs was -en (never -e).

APPENDIX

MIDDLE ENGLISH SPELLING

88. Influence of Old English Spelling. In the beginning of the Middle English period (roughly between 1050 and 1150) there occurred a large number of changes of pronunciation, particularly in the vowel sounds. Old English æ became [a]; Old English ā became [ǭ]; the Old English diphthongs ēa, ea, ēo, and eo became the simple vowels [ę̄], [a], [ē] and [ę]; and a number of new diphthongs—[ai], [ęi], [au], etc.—developed out of Old English simple vowels followed by ġ, w, h, etc.[94] While these changes were going on and for some time after they had been carried out, people continued to spell words in the way they had been spelled in Old English. For example, Old English þæt was spelled with æ, Old English bēon[95] was spelled with eo, Old English strēam was spelled with ea, and Old English stān was spelled with a after the pronunciation of these words had become [þat], [bēn], [strę̄m], and [stǭn]. But the changes that had taken place in pronunciation were so numerous that it proved to be impossible to maintain the old system of spelling. Confusion in spelling soon arose. Since words that were spelled with eo and with e came to have the same sound in Middle English, people regarded the two signs as interchangeable; they would therefore spell Old English bēon and weorc with e, and Old English swēte and helpan with eo. Moreover, ea and eo were enough alike in appearance to be confused in use, so that [bēn], from Old English bēon was sometimes spelled with ea and [strę̄m], from Old English strēam was sometimes spelled with eo. As a result, the spelling of the vowel sounds in the earliest Middle

---

[94] For an account of these sound changes see 42, 43, 46 above.

[95] The Old English manuscripts as a rule make no distinction between long and short vowels and diphthongs; bēon, for example, with a long diphthong, and weorc, with a short diphthong, are both spelled with eo. The marks of length are added by modern editors. Nor do the manuscripts distinguish ċ (i.e., [tʃ]) from c (i.e., [k]) or ġ (i.e., [j]) from g (i.e., [g]). The dot is added by modern editors.

English texts exhibits great confusion, which gradually diminished, however, as the digraphs ea and eo fell more and more into disuse and as the character æ gave place to a as a means of representing the vowel [a].

89. Influence of Old French Spelling. There is no doubt that in the course of time the confusion of early Middle English spelling would have been done away with and that a good system of spelling Middle English would have been evolved on the basis of the Old English system if the English people had been left to themselves. But they were not left to themselves. French was the language of the superior class from 1066 to the middle of the fourteenth century. Educated people read French books and were expected to be able to write as well as speak the French language; French words were adopted into the language and kept their French spellings when used in writing. As a result, people began to spell certain English sounds according to the French system of spelling. The most important changes that came about were these:

1. $[\bar{ę}]$, spelled in OE with æ and in early ME with æ or ea, came to be spelled with e, as in French; e.g., early ME **hæþ**, later ME **heþ** or **heeth**.
2. [u], spelled in OE and early ME with u, was often spelled with o in later ME, particularly in proximity with letters like n, m, v, and w; e.g., early ME **sune**, later ME **sone**.
3. $[\bar{u}]$, spelled in OE and early ME with u, was usually spelled in late ME with ou; e.g., early ME **hus**, late ME **hous**.
4. [y] and $[\bar{y}]$, which were spelled in OE with y and had the sound of French u, were spelled in Southern ME with u, as in French; $[\bar{y}]$ was sometimes spelled ui; e.g., OE **fyllan**, Southern ME **vulle(n)**; OE **fȳr**, Southern ME **vur, vuir**.
5. $[\bar{e}]$, spelled in early ME with e or eo is often spelled in late ME with ie; e.g., OE **spēdan**, early ME **spede(n)**, late ME **spede(n)** or **spiede(n)**.
6. [v], spelled in OE and in the earliest ME with f, came to be spelled with v, as in French; e.g., OE **life**, ME **live**.
7. [tʃ], spelled in OE with c, came to be spelled in ME with ch, as in French; e.g., OE **čidan**,[x] ME **chide(n)**.
8. [kw], spelled in OE with cw, came to be spelled in ME with qu, as in French; e.g., OE **cwēn**, ME **quen** or **queen**.

[x] As to č, see the preceding note.

The influence of French spelling on English spelling began soon after the Norman conquest, but the changes which it brought about were not completed until after the middle of the thirteenth century.

90. Spelling of Middle English Vowels and Diphthongs. The table given below shows the spellings which are most commonly used in Middle English manuscripts to represent the various vowels and diphthongs The first column contains the sounds as represented in phonetic notation; the second column contains the spellings by which these sounds are represented in the earlier Middle English manuscripts (roughly, before 1250); the third column contains the spellings by which these same sounds are represented in the later Middle English manuscripts (roughly, after 1250). Spellings which are decidedly less frequent than the others are placed in parentheses.

ME Sound	Early ME Spelling	Late ME Spelling
[ā][97]		a, aa
[a]	a, æ, ea	a
[ē]	e, eo	e, ee, (ie)
[ę̄]	æ, ea, e, (eo)	e, ee
[e]	e, eo, (æ)	e
[ī]	i, (y)	i, ii, y
[i]	i, (y)	i, y
[ō]	o	o, oo
[ǭ]	a, o, (oa)	o, oo
[o]	o	o
[ū]	u, v[98]	ou, (o)
[u]	u, v	u, v, o
[ȳ]	u, v, ui	u, v, ui
[y]	u, v	u, v
[ai]	ai, æi, ei, aȝ, æȝ[99]	
[au]	au, aw, aȝ, aᵹ, agh	au, aw
[ęi]	ei, æi, eȝ, æȝ	ei, ai, ey, ay

[97] [ā] does not occur in the earliest ME, for the OE [ā] became [ǭ] in ME. The ME [ā] was the result of the lengthening of [a] in open syllables; see 43, 1b above and note 43b.

[98] The letters u and v were used interchangeably by the Middle English scribes.

[99] The diphthong [ai] occurs only in early ME; in late ME it became identical in sound with [ęi].

ME Sound	Early ME Spelling	Late ME Spelling
[eu]	eu, ew	eu, ew
[iu]	iu, iw, eu, ew, eou, eow	iu, iw, eu, ew, u, ui
[ǫu]	au, aw, aȝ, ag, agh, ou, ow, oȝ, og, ogh[100]	ou, ow
[ou]	ou, ow, o	ou, ow, o
[oi][101]		oi, oy, (ui)[102]

The student should remember that all diacritical marks which he finds in Middle English texts are supplied by modern editors.

91. Spelling of Middle English Consonants. The table given below shows the spellings which are most commonly used in Middle English manuscripts to represent consonant sounds, so far as the spelling of these sounds differs from that of Modern English.

ME Sound	EME Spelling	LME Spelling
[h][103]	h, ȝ,[104] g	gh, h, ȝ, ch
[hw]	hw, wh	wh
[j]	ȝ,[104] g	y, ȝ

[100] The Middle English diphthongs are variously spelled in early Middle English for two reasons. First, the sounds of which they were composed were variously spelled, [ǭ], e.g., being spelled either a or o. Second, the diphthongs themselves were of various origin (see 43, 2 above), [au], e.g., developing out of OE a followed by w or g, or out of OE ea followed by h. Many of the early Middle English spellings of these diphthongs are etymological spellings which do not represent adequately the true nature of the sounds. See also note 104 below.

[101] The diphthong [oi] occurs only rarely in early Middle English; it is therefore given only in the third column.

[102] The tables given in 90 and 91 are not intended to include all of the spellings that occur in Middle English manuscripts, but only those that are fairly common. No account is taken of spellings that are rare or eccentric. And no account is taken of spellings that may represent differences of pronunciation; such spellings are dealt with in the account of Middle English dialects which is given in 81 ff.

[103] That is, [h] before consonants and after vowels.

[104] The character ȝ was called ȝoȝ [jǫh], and was a slight modification of the Old English form of the letter g. The Old English g represented two sounds, that of [j], e.g., in dæġ, and that of [ɣ], e.g., in āgen; this sound is a spirant like the g of North German sagen. In Middle English the sound of [j] was preserved if it occurred at the beginning of a word, as in ȝe, from OE ġē. But when it was preceded by a vowel it united with the vowel to form a diphthong, as in ME dai from OE dæġ. The Old English sound [ɣ] became [w] in early ME when it was preceded by a vowel, and then it united with the preceding vowel to form a diphthong, as in ME owen [ǭuən] from

ME Sound	EME Spelling	LME Spelling
[ʃ]	sc, ss, s	sch, ssch, sh, ssh
[þ]	þ,[105] ð[106]	þ, th
[ð]	þ, ð	þ, th
[v]	f, v, u	v, u
[w]	w (initially)	w
[w]	w, ȝ, g, gh (medially)[107]	w

OE āgen. In the few words in which it was followed by a vowel and preceded by a consonant, OE [ʒ] became [w] in ME, e.g., in halwien, from OE hālgian. OE initial [ʒ] however, became in ME a stop consonant like the g in Modern English good. This stop g was then spelled with a new variety of the letter g which was very much like the modern g. The Old English form of the letter g, slightly modified, was then used to spell the sounds other than stop g which had developed out of the two Old English sounds of g. That is, it was used to represent:

1. The sound of [j], e.g., in ȝe, from OE ȝē;
2. The sound of [w], e.g., in halȝien, from OE hālgian;
3. The second element of the diphthongs [ai] and [ei], e.g., in daȝ from OE dæg and weȝ from OE weg;
4. The second element of the diphthongs [au] and [ōu], e.g., in draȝen from OE dragan and aȝen or oȝen from OE āgen.

It was also used to represent:

5. The sound of [h] before consonants and after vowels, e.g., in niȝt from OE niht.

[105] The name of the letter þ is "thorn."

[106] The name of the letter ð is "crossed d" or "eth" [eð].

[107] [w] is spelled ȝ or gh when it developed out of OE [ʒ], e.g., in halȝien, halghien from OE hālgian. See note 104 above.

LaVergne, TN USA
10 February 2011
215997LV00003B/154/P